Prayers
for Pastor
& People

Prayers for Pastor & People

Compiled and edited by
Carl G. Carlozzi, D. Min.

With a Foreword by
The Rt. Rev. John B. Coburn, D.D., S.T.D.

 CHURCH

Church Publishing Incorporated, New York

Church Publishing Incorporated
445 Fifth Avenue
New York NY 10016

ISBN 0-89869-108-7

Foreword

When the author of this book, *Prayers for Pastor and People*, was a student at the Episcopal Theological School in the nineteen-sixties, he once submitted as a term paper in a course on prayer, which I was teaching, a series of prayers that so impressed me that I urged him to try to have them published and, even if they were not, to keep on writing. Unlike some other students I have had, he followed my advice!

He seemed to me then to be a young man "haunted by prayer." He has consistently throughout his ministry continued to be so haunted — which is to be "haunted by God" — and this volume is the result. Any pastor of any denomination can be thankful that he has persisted in this special vocation because there is now made available an unusually rich deposit of prayers for every conceivable pastoral situation.

This is a compilation of prayers which draws upon the heritage of Anglican spirituality (both personal and corporate) and is so catholic that it can be used by pastors of any Christian persuasion. It is resource material classified into ten categories ranging from "Community, Nation, and World" to "General Intercessions and Bidding Prayers." The editing has been done with care; the sources are identified precisely and an excellent index is provided.

All in all, this is a most useful reference work for the pastor to keep near at hand in the preparation of services of worship and to meet the needs of his or her people. I am happy to commend it as (in my judgment) the best volume of its kind for the present generation of pastors — and their people.

John B. Coburn
Boston, Massachusetts
11 November, 1983

Contents

Source Designation Key

[296]
Page 296 in *The Book of Common Prayer*, 1979, The Church Hymnal Corporation, New York, N.Y.

[28BCP, 182]
Page 182 in *The Book of Common Prayer*, 1928, The Church Hymnal Corporation, New York, N.Y.

[BOOS, 130]
Page 130 in *The Book of Occasional Services*, The Church Hymnal Corporation, New York, N.Y., 1979.

[LFF, 16]
Page 16 in *Lesser Feasts and Fasts*, The Church Hymnal Corporation, New York, N.Y., 1980.

[MFP, 178]
Page 178 in *A Manual For Priests*, Society of Saint John The Evangelist, Cambridge, MA., 1970.

[SAPB, 54]
Page 54 in *Saint Augustine's Prayer Book*, The Order of the Holy Cross, West Park, N.Y., 1976.

[PPB, NO. 545]
Prayer number 545 in *The Pastor's Prayerbook*, Robert N. Rodenmayer, Editor, Oxford University Press, New York, N.Y., 1960.

[DCS]
Composed by The Rev. Douglas C. Smith, Associate Priest, All Saints' Church, Phoenix, AZ.

[PTL, 93]
Page 93 in *Prayers, Thanksgivings, and Litanies*, The Church Hymnal Corporation, New York, N.Y., 1973.

[_____][43]
See Footnote 43 in back of book.

Preface

This book of prayers, based in the rich heritage and treasury of the Anglican tradition, is offered to the Glory of God and to pastors and people of all Christian denominations. It is hoped this volume will be of assistance to clergy in providing for a more comprehensive offering of prayers in corporate worship and to Christian people everywhere as they seek to enhance their own personal devotional lives.

I am deeply indebted to the thousands of faithful followers of Christ, known and unknown, whose labors of literary creativity, through the inspiration of the Spirit, have made this book possible, especially those whose devotional genius contributed to present and past editions of *The Book of Common Prayer* of the Episcopal Church.

Further, in the use of prayers from source books which are under copyright, every attempt has been made to credit original writers. In particular, special thanks are due to the following who have graciously granted permission to reprint prayers from their volumes: The Societyof Saint John The Evangelist, Cambridge, Massachusetts, for prayers in *A Manual For Priests*; The Order of the Holy Cross, West Park, New York for prayers in *Saint Augustine's Prayer Book*; Oxford University Press, New York, for prayers in *The Pastor's Prayerbook*, Robert N. Rodenmayer, editor; and The Church Hymnal Corporation, New York, for prayers in *The Book of Occasional Services*, and *Prayers, Thanksgivings, and Litanies*, and *Lesser Feasts and Fasts*. In addition, I would like to thank my associate, The Rev. Douglas C. Smith, for his own creative contributions.

Finally, I wish to express my appreciation to the following: The Rev. Marion J. Hatchett for his kind research assistance relative to the 1928 *Book of Common Prayer*; The Rev. W. Ray Worthington for allowing me full access to his library; Mr. David Baker for his computer expertise in the compiling of the index; and last of all, the wardens, vestry and people of All Saints' Church and Day School for granting me the study leave to undertake and complete this project.

May the gracious Lord who hears our prayers grant *you* the power of his Spirit and an ever abiding sense of his presence in *your* life this day and forever.

Carl G. Carlozzi, D. Min.
Phoenix, Arizona
September, 1983

I
Community, Nation and World

Community, Nation and World

For the president and civil authorities

O Lord our Governor, whose glory is in all the world: We
commend this nation to your merciful care, that being guided
by your Providence, we may dwell secure in your peace.
Grant to the President of the United States, the Governor
of this State (*or* commonwealth), and to all in authority,
wisdom and strength to know and to do your will. Fill them
with the love of truth and righteousness, and make them ever
mindful of their calling to serve this people in your fear;
through Jesus Christ our Lord, who lives and reigns with you
and the Holy Spirit, one God, world without end.
Amen.   [820]

Almighty God, whose kingdom is everlasting and power
infinite; Have mercy upon this whole land; and so rule the
hearts of thy servants THE PRESIDENT OF THE UNITED
STATES, *The Governor of this State*, and all others in
authority, that they, knowing whose ministers they are, may
above all things seek thy honor and glory; and that we and
all the People, duly considering whose authority they bear,
may faithfully and obediently honor them, according to thy
blessed Word and ordinance; through Jesus Christ our Lord,
who with thee and the Holy Ghost liveth and reigneth ever,
one God, world without end. *Amen.*   [28BCP, 132]

O Lord, our heavenly Father, the high and mighty Ruler of the universe, who dost from thy throne behold all the dwellers upon earth; Most heartily we beseech thee, with thy favor to behold and bless thy servant THE PRESIDENT OF THE UNITED STATES, and all others in authority; and so replenish them with the grace of thy Holy Spirit, that they may always incline to thy will, and walk in thy way. Endue them plenteously with heavenly gifts; grant them in health and prosperity long to live; and finally, after this life, to attain everlasting joy and felicity; through Jesus Christ our Lord. *Amen.* [28BCP, 17]

For the human family

O God, you made us in your own image and redeemed us through Jesus your Son: Look with compassion on the whole human family; take away the arrogance and hatred which infect our hearts; break down the walls that separate us; unite us in bonds of love; and work through our struggle and confusion to accomplish your purposes on earth; that, in your good time, all nations and races may serve you in harmony around your heavenly throne; through Jesus Christ our Lord. *Amen* [815]

For the future of the human race

O God our heavenly Father, you have blessed us and given us dominion over all the earth: Increase our reverence before the mystery of life; and give us new insight into your purposes for the human race, and new wisdom and determination in making provision for its future in accordance with your will; through Jesus Christ our Lord. *Amen.* [828]

In time of an epidemic

O most mighty and merciful God, in this time of grievous sickness, we flee unto thee for succor. Deliver us, we beseech thee, from our peril; give strength and skill to all those who minister to the sick; prosper the means made use of for their cure; and grant that, perceiving how frail and uncertain our life is, we may apply our hearts unto that heavenly wisdom which leadeth to eternal life; through Jesus Christ our Lord. *Amen.* [28BCP, 45]

For innocent victims

We remember today, O God, the slaughter of the holy innocents of Bethlehem by King Herod. Receive, we pray, into the arms of your mercy all innocent victims; and by your great might frustrate the designs of evil tyrants and establish your rule of justice, love, and peace; through Jesus Christ our Lord, who lives and reigns with you, in the unity of the Holy Spirit, one God, for ever and ever. *Amen.* [238]

For cities

Heavenly Father, in your Word you have given us a vision of that holy City to which the nations of the world bring their glory: Behold and visit, we pray, the cities of the earth. Renew the ties of mutual regard which form our civic life. Send us honest and able leaders. Enable us to eliminate poverty, prejudice, and oppression, that peace may prevail with righteousness, and justice with order, and that men and women from different cultures and with differing talents may find with one another the fulfillment of their humanity; through Jesus Christ our Lord. *Amen.* [825]

For commerce and industry

Almighty God, whose Son Jesus Christ in his earthly life
shared our toil and hallowed our labor: Be present with
your people where they work; make those who carry on the
industries and commerce of this land responsive to your will;
and give to us all a pride in what we do, and a just return for
our labor; through Jesus Christ our Lord, who lives and
reigns with you, in the unity of the Holy Spirit, one God,
now and for ever. *Amen.*   [259]

For working toward the common good

Almighty God, you have so linked our lives one with
another that all we do affects, for good or ill, all other lives:
So guide us in the work we do, that we may do it not for self
alone, but for the common good; and, as we seek a proper
return for our own labor, make us mindful of the rightful
aspirations of other workers, and arouse our concern for
those who are out of work; through Jesus Christ our Lord,
who lives and reigns with you and the Holy Spirit, one God,
for ever and ever. *Amen.*   [261]

In times of conflict

O God, you have bound us together in a common life. Help
us, in the midst of our struggles for justice and truth, to
confront one another without hatred or bitterness, and to
work together with mutual forbearance and respect; through
Jesus Christ our Lord. *Amen.*   [824]

For our country

Almighty God, who hast given us this good land for our
heritage: We humbly beseech thee that we may always prove
ourselves a people mindful of thy favor and glad to do thy

will. Bless our land with honorable industry, sound learning, and pure manners. Save us from violence, discord, and confusion; from pride and arrogance, and from every evil way. Defend our liberties, and fashion into one united people the multitudes brought hither out of many kindreds and tongues. Endue with the spirit of wisdom those to whom in thy Name we entrust the authority of government, that there may be justice and peace at home, and that, through obedience to thy law, we may show forth thy praise among the nations of the earth. In the time of prosperity, fill our hearts with thankfulness, and in the day of trouble, suffer not our trust in thee to fail; all which we ask through Jesus Christ our Lord. *Amen.* [820]

Almighty God, the source of all life, giver of all blessing, and savior of all who turn to you: Have mercy upon this nation; deliver us from falsehood, malice, and disobedience; turn our feet into your paths; and grant that we may serve you in peace; through Jesus Christ our Lord. *Amen.* [BOOS, 41]

In time of calamity

O God, merciful and compassionate, who art ever ready to hear the prayers of those who put their trust in thee; Graciously hearken to us who call upon thee, and grant us thy help in this our need; through Jesus Christ our Lord. *Amen.* [28BCP, 41]

For fellow-citizens abroad

Watch over our fellow-citizens, O Lord, who live and travel in other lands. Open them to the values of different cultures, and make them worthy representatives of our own, that by their courtesy and good judgment they may strengthen the bonds of friendship and peace; through Jesus Christ our Lord. *Amen.* [PTL, 45][1]

For peace

Eternal God, in whose perfect kingdom no sword is drawn
but the sword of righteousness, no strength known but the
strength of love: So mightily spread abroad your Spirit, that
all peoples may be gathered under the banner of the Prince of
Peace, as children of one Father; to whom be dominion and
glory, now and for ever. *Amen.*   [815]

Almighty God our heavenly Father, guide the nations of the
world into the way of justice and truth, and establish among
them that peace which is the fruit of righteousness, that they
may become the kingdom of our Lord and Savior Jesus
Christ. *Amen.*   [816]

Almighty God, whose will it is to hold both heaven and earth
in the peace of your kingdom: Give peace to your Church,
peace among nations, peace in our homes, and peace in our
hearts; through your Son, our Savior, Jesus Christ.
Amen.   [PTL, 30]²

For those who influence public opinion

Almighty God, you proclaim your truth in every age by
many voices: Direct, in our time, we pray, those who speak
where many listen and write what many read; that they may
do their part in making the heart of this people wise, its mind
sound, and its will righteous; to the honor of Jesus Christ our
Lord. *Amen.*   [827]

For rain

O God, heavenly Father, who by your Son Jesus Christ
has promised to all those who seek your kingdom and its
righteousness all things necessary to sustain their life: Send
us, we entreat you, in this time of need, such moderate rain

and showers, that we may receive the fruits of the earth, to our comfort and to your honor; through Jesus Christ our Lord. *Amen.* [828]

For the poor and neglected

Almighty and most merciful God, we remember before you all poor and neglected persons whom it would be easy for us to forget: the homeless and the destitute, the old and the sick, and all who have none to care for them. Help us to heal those who are broken in body or spirit, and to turn their sorrow into joy. Grant this, Father, for the love of your Son, who for our sake became poor, Jesus Christ our Lord. *Amen.* [826]

O God, Almighty and merciful, who healest those that are broken in heart, and turnest the sadness of the sorrowful to joy; Let thy fatherly goodness be upon all that thou hast made. Remember in pity such as are this day destitute, homeless, or forgotten of their fellow-men. Bless the congregation of thy poor. Uplift those who are cast down. Mightily befriend innocent sufferers, and sanctify to them the endurance of their wrongs. Cheer with hope all discouraged and unhappy people, and by thy heavenly grace preserve from falling those whose penury tempteth them to sin; though they be troubled on every side, suffer them not to be distressed; though they be perplexed, save them from despair. Grant this, O Lord, for the love of him, who for our sakes became poor, thy Son, our Savior Jesus Christ. *Amen.* [28BCP, 599]

For the conservation of natural resources

Almighty God, in giving us dominion over things on earth, you made us fellow workers in your creation: Give us wisdom and reverence so to use the resources of nature, that no one may suffer from our abuse of them, and that generations yet to come may continue to praise you for your bounty; through Jesus Christ our Lord. *Amen.* [827]

Almighty God, whose loving hand hath given us all that we possess; Grant us grace that we may honor thee with our substance, and remembering the account which we must one day give, may be faithful stewards of thy bounty; through Jesus Christ our Lord. *Amen.* [28BCP, 599]

A general intercession

O God, at whose word man goeth forth to his work and to his labor until the evening; Be merciful to all whose duties are difficult or burdensome, and comfort them concerning their toil. Shield from bodily accident and harm the workmen at their work. Protect the efforts of sober and honest industry, and suffer not the hire of the laborers to be kept back by fraud. Incline the heart of employers and of those whom they employ to mutual forbearance, fairness, and good-will. Give the spirit of governance and of a sound mind to all in places of authority. Bless all those who labor in works of mercy or in schools of good learning. Care for all aged persons, and all little children, the sick and the afflicted, and those who travel by land or by sea. Remember all who by reason of weakness are overtasked, or because of poverty are forgotten. Let the sorrowful sighing of the prisoners come before thee; and according to the greatness of thy power, preserve thou those that are appointed to die. Give ear unto our prayer, O merciful and gracious father, for the love of thy dear Son, our Savior Jesus Christ. *Amen.*
[28BCP, 599]

For a spirit of reconciliation

Lord, make us instruments of your peace. Where there
is hatred, let us sow love; where there is injury, pardon;
where there is discord, union; where there is doubt, faith;
where there is despair, hope; where there is darkness, light;
where there is sadness, joy. Grant that we may not so much
seek to be consoled as to console; to be understood as to
understand; to be loved as to love. For it is in giving that we
receive; it is in pardoning that we are pardoned; and it is in
dying that we are born to eternal life. *Amen.* [833]

For the church in a changing world

O God, sustain your Church as we face new tasks in the
confusions of this changing world. By your Holy Spirit give
us good judgment and the strength to persevere, so that we
may boldly bear witness to the coming of your kingdom;
through Jesus Christ our Lord. *Amen.* [PTL, 36][3]

For the navy

O Eternal Lord God, who alone spreadest out the heavens,
and rulest the raging of the sea; Vouchsafe to take into thy
almighty and most gracious protection our country's Navy,
and all who serve therein. Preserve them from the dangers of
the sea, and from the violence of the enemy; that they may be
a safeguard unto the United States of America, and a security
for such as pass on the seas upon their lawful occasions; that
the inhabitants of our land may in peace and quietness serve
thee our God, to the glory of thy Name; through Jesus Christ
our Lord. *Amen.* [28BCP, 42]

For animals

O God, you created all living things on the face of the earth and gave us dominion over them: Grant that we may be faithful to this trust in the way we treat all animals, both wild and tame. Teach us to admire their beauty and to delight in their cunning; to respect their strength and to wonder at their intelligence. Grant that our use of them may be both merciful and wise. So may we lend our voice to their praise of your goodness, which endures for ever. *Amen.*   [PTL, 55]¹

For the responsible use of inventions and discoveries

Almighty and merciful God, without you all things hasten to destruction and fall into nothingness: Look upon us now with compassion, for we have learned to unlock power from atoms and lift ourselves into the boundless space of your creation. Save us, lest we abuse these discoveries which you have put into our hands, turning them to the world's misery and ruin. Teach us to think your thoughts after you in fear and wonder, and to use our knowledge for man's welfare and to your glory; through Jesus Christ our Lord. *Amen.*   [PTL, 54]⁴

For a person, or persons, going to sea

O Eternal God, who alone spreadest out the heavens, and rulest the raging of the sea; We commend to thy almighty protection, thy *servant*, for whose preservation on the great deep our prayers are desired. Guard *him*, we beseech thee, from the dangers of the sea, from sickness, from the violence of enemies, and from every evil to which *he* may be exposed. Conduct *him* in safety to the haven where *he* would be, with a grateful sense of thy mercies; through Jesus Christ our Lord. *Amen.*   [28BCP, 46]

For children

Almighty God, whose compassion embraces all men, we beseech you for the world's children. May those whose small bodies are undernourished or diseased be fed and made whole; May those whose minds are dull and unchallenged come alive; May those whose homes are broken by strife find peace and security. Protect in all children, O Lord, their special sponteneity; and keep from despair those who know failure or frustration. In due time bring them, your children and our brothers, to their full human stature; through Jesus Christ our Lord. *Amen.*   [PTL, 57][5]

For prisoners

O God, who sparest when we deserve punishment, and in thy wrath rememberest mercy; We humbly beseech thee, of thy goodness, to comfort and succor all prisoners (*especially those who are condemned to die*). Give them a right understanding of themselves, and of thy promises; that, trusting wholly in thy mercy, they may not place their confidence anywhere but in thee. Relieve the distressed, protect the innocent, awaken the guilty; and forasmuch as thou alone bringest light out of darkness, and good out of evil, grant to these thy servants, that by the power of thy Holy Spirit they may be set free from the chains of sin, and may be brought to newness of life; through Jesus Christ our Lord. *Amen.*   [28BCP, 46]

For all sorts and conditions of men

O God, the creator and preserver of all mankind, we humbly beseech thee for all sorts and conditions of men; that thou wouldest be pleased to make thy ways known unto them, thy saving health unto all nations. More especially we pray for thy holy Church universal; that it may be so guided and governed by thy good Spirit, that all who profess and call themselves Christians may be led into the way of truth, and hold the faith in unity of spirit, in the bond of peace, and in righteousness of life. Finally, we commend to thy fatherly goodness all those who are in any ways afflicted or distressed, in mind, body, or estate; (especially those for whom our prayers are desired); that it may please thee to comfort and relieve them according to their several necessities, giving them patience under their sufferings, and a happy issue out of all their afflictions. And this we beg for Jesus Christ's sake. *Amen.* [814]

For those who live alone

Almighty God, whose Son had nowhere to lay his head: Grant that those who live alone may not be lonely in their solitude, but that, following in his steps, they may find fulfillment in loving you and their neighbors; through Jesus Christ our Lord. *Amen.* [829]

For those in the armed forces

Almighty God, we commend to your gracious care and keeping all the men and women of our armed forces at home and abroad. Defend them day by day with your heavenly grace; strengthen them in their trials and temptations; give them courage to face the perils which beset them; and grant them a sense of your abiding presence wherever they may be; through Jesus Christ our Lord. *Amen.* [823]

For our enemies

O God, the Father of all, whose Son commanded us to love our enemies: Lead them and us from prejudice to truth;

deliver them and us from hatred, cruelty, and revenge; and in your good time enable us all to stand reconciled before you; through Jesus Christ our Lord. *Amen.*   [816]

For education

Almighty God, the fountain of all wisdom: Enlighten by your Holy Spirit those who teach and those who learn, that, rejoicing in the knowledge of your truth, they may worship you and serve you from generation to generation; through Jesus Christ our Lord, who lives and reigns with you and the Holy Spirit, one God, for ever and ever. *Amen.*   [261]

For those who do not know Christ

Merciful God, creator of all the peoples of the earth and lover of souls: have compassion on all who do not know you as you are revealed in your Son Jesus Christ; let your Gospel be preached with grace and power to those who have not heard it; turn the hearts of those who resist it; and bring home to your fold those who have gone astray; that there may be one flock under one shepherd, Jesus Christ our Lord. *Amen.*   [280]

For the oppressed

Look with pity, O heavenly Father, upon the people in this land who live with injustice, terror, disease, and death as their constant companions. Have mercy upon us. Help us to eliminate our cruelty to these our neighbors. Strengthen those who spend their lives establishing equal protection of the law and equal opportunities for all. And grant that every one of us may enjoy a fair portion of the riches of this land; through Jesus Christ our Lord. *Amen.*   [826]

For the accomplishment of God's will

Grant that the bonds of our common humanity, by which all your children are united one to another, and the living to the dead, may be so transformed by your grace, that your will may be done on earth as it is in heaven; where, O Father, with your Son and the Holy Spirit, you live and reign in perfect unity, now and for ever. *Amen.* [430]

For fruitful seasons

Almighty God, Lord of heaven and earth: We humbly pray that your gracious providence may give and preserve to our use the harvests of the land and of the seas, and may prosper all who labor to gather them, that we, who are constantly receiving good things from your hand, may always give you thanks; through Jesus Christ our Lord, who lives and reigns with you and the Holy Spirit, one God, for ever and ever. *Amen.* [258]

For joy in God's creation

O heavenly Father, who has filled the world with beauty: Open our eyes to behold your gracious hand in all your works; that, rejoicing in your whole creation, we may learn to serve you with gladness; for the sake of him through whom all things were made, your Son Jesus Christ our Lord. *Amen.* [814]

For local government

Almighty God our heavenly Father, send down upon those who hold office in this state (commonwealth, city, county, town, _____) the spirit of wisdom, charity, and justice; that with steadfast purpose they may faithfully serve in their offices to promote the well-being of all people; through Jesus Christ our Lord. *Amen.*   [822]

For world order

O God and Father of all, whom the whole heavens adore: Let the whole earth also worship you, all nations obey you, all tongues confess and bless you, and men and women everywhere love you and serve you in peace; through Jesus Christ our Lord. *Amen.*   [124]

For travellers

O God, our heavenly Father, whose glory fills the whole creation, and whose presence we find wherever we go: Preserve those who travel (in particular _____); surround them with your loving care; protect them from every danger; and bring them in safety to their journey's end; through Jesus Christ our Lord. *Amen.*   [831]

For the unemployed

Heavenly Father, we remember before you those who suffer want and anxiety from lack of work. Guide the people of this land so to use our public and private wealth that all may find suitable and fulfilling employment, and receive just payment for their labor; through Jesus Christ our Lord. *Amen.*   [824]

For world evangelical outreach

Give us grace, O Lord, to answer readily the call of our Savior Jesus Christ and proclaim to all people the Good News of his salvation, that we and the whole world may perceive the glory of his marvelous works; who lives and reigns with you and the Holy Spirit, one God, for ever and ever. *Amen.* [215]

For world leaders

Almighty God, kindle, we pray, in every heart the true love of peace, and guide with your wisdom those who take counsel for the nations of the earth; that in tranquillity your dominion may increase, until the earth is filled with the knowledge of your love; through Jesus Christ our Lord. *Amen.*   [278]

For rural areas

Lord Christ, when you came among us, you proclaimed the kingdom of God in villages, towns, and lonely places: Grant that your presence and power may be known throughout this land. Have mercy upon all of us who live and work in rural areas (especially _____); and grant that all the people of our nation may give thanks to you for food and drink and all other bodily necessities of life, respect those who labor to produce them, and honor the land and the water from which these good things come. All this we ask in your holy Name. *Amen.*   [825]

For schools and colleges

O Eternal God, bless all schools, colleges, and universities (and especially _____), that they may be lively centers for sound learning, new discovery, and the pursuit of wisdom; and grant that those who teach and those who learn may find you to be the source of all truth; through Jesus Christ our Lord. *Amen.*   [824]

For sinful humanity

Almighty and everlasting God, whose will it is to restore all things in your well-beloved Son, the King of kings and Lord of lords: Mercifully grant that the peoples of the earth, divided and enslaved by sin, may be freed and brought together under his most gracious rule; who lives and reigns with you and the Holy Spirit, one God, now and for ever. *Amen.* [236]

For social justice

Almighty God, who created us in your own image: Grant us grace fearlessly to contend against evil and to make no peace with oppression; and, that we may reverently use our freedom, help us to employ it in the maintenance of justice in our communities and among the nations, to the glory of your holy Name; through Jesus Christ our Lord, who lives and reigns with you and the Holy Spirit, one God, now and for ever. *Amen.* [260]

For young persons

God our Father, you see your children growing up in an unsteady and confusing world: Show them that your ways give more life than the ways of the world, and that following you is better than chasing after selfish goals. Help them to take failure, not as a measure of their worth, but as a chance for a new start. Give them strength to hold their faith in you, and to keep alive their joy in your creation; through Jesus Christ our Lord. *Amen.* [829]

For the harvest of lands and waters

O gracious Father, who opens your hand and fills all things living with plenteousness: Bless the lands and waters, and multiply the harvests of the world; let your Spirit go forth, that it may renew the face of the earth; show your loving-kindness, that our land may give her increase; and save us from selfish use of what you give, that men and women everywhere may give you thanks; through Jesus Christ our lord. *Amen.* [828]

For correctional institutions

Lord Jesus, for our sake you were condemned as a criminal:
Visit our jails and prisons with your pity and judgment.
Remember all prisoners, and bring the guilty to repentance
and amendment of life according to your will, and give them
hope for their future. When any are held unjustly, bring them
release; forgive us, and teach us to improve our justice.
Remember those who work in these institutions; keep them
humane and compassionate; and save them from becoming
brutal or callous. And since what we do for those in prison,
O Lord, we do for you, constrain us to improve their lot. All
this we ask for your mercy's sake. *Amen.*   [826]

For congress or a state legislature

O God, the fountain of wisdom, whose will is good and
gracious, and whose law is truth: We beseech you so
to guide and bless our senators and representatives in
congress assembled (*or* in the legislature of this state,
or commonwealth), that they may enact such laws as shall
please you, to the glory of your Name and the welfare of
this people; through Jesus Christ our Lord. *Amen.*   [821]

Most gracious God, we humbly beseech thee, as for the
people of these United States in general, so especially for
their senate and representatives in congress assembled; that
thou wouldest be pleased to direct and prosper all their
consultations, to the advancement of thy glory, the good of
thy Church, the safety, honor, and welfare of thy people; that
all things may be so ordered and settled by their endeavors,
upon the best and surest foundations, that peace and
happiness, truth and justice, religion and piety, may be
established among us for all generations. These and all other
necessaries, for them, for us, and thy whole Church, we
humbly beg in the Name and mediation of Jesus Christ, our
most blessed Lord and Savior. *Amen.*   [28BCP, 35]

O God, the fountain of wisdom, whose statutes are good and gracious and whose law is truth; We beseech thee so to guide and bless the legislature of this state, that it may ordain for our governance only such things as please thee, to the glory of thy Name and the welfare of the people; through Jesus Christ, thy Son, our Lord. *Amen.*   [28BCP, 35]

For the family of nations

Almighty God, our heavenly Father, guide, we beseech thee, the Nations of the world into the way of justice and truth, and establish among them that peace which is the fruit of righteousness, that they may become the Kingdom of our Lord and Savior Jesus Christ. *Amen.*   [28BCP, 44]

In time of industrial strife

O God, who willest that men should live and work together as brethren: we beseech thee to remove the spirit of strife and selfishness from those who are now at variance; that seeking only what is just they may ever abide in brotherly union and concord, to their own well-being and the good of all mankind; through Jesus Christ our Lord. *Amen.*   [MFP, 270]

In time of war

O Almighty God, who art a most strong tower to all who put their trust in thee: Be now and evermore our defence; grant us victory, if it be thy will; look in pity upon the wounded and the prisoners; cheer the anxious; comfort the bereaved; succor the dying; have mercy upon the fallen; and hasten the time when war shall cease in all the world; through Jesus Christ our Lord. *Amen.*   [MFP, 270]

Before an athletic contest

O Almighty God, who alone art the final judge of life's great race: be with this our N. team in its contest of sporting skill, and grant that should we win we may accept our victory humbly; or should we be defeated we may take our loss graciously; through Jesus Christ our Lord. *Amen.*
[MFP, 273]

For teachers

Almighty Father, who didst send thine only Son, that through him all men might be saved: So consecrate the lives of those whom thou dost call to teach, that, being themselves led by thee, they may lead their pupils in the paths of everlasting life; through the same our Lord and Savior Jesus Christ. *Amen.*   [MFP, 273]

For hospitals and healing ministries

Almighty God, whose blessed Son Jesus Christ went about healing all manner of sickness among the people: Continue, we pray, his gracious work among us; bless and provide for our hospitals; grant to physicians, surgeons, nurses and all who serve with them, wisdom and skill, sympathy and patience; and give your blessing to all who work to prevent suffering; through Jesus Christ our Lord. *Amen.*   [PTL, 63][6]

For the exploration of space

O God, who hast created the heavens and the earth: guide and preserve those who penetrate the vastness of outer space; and grant that we who learn from their explorations may come to perceive the majesty of thy creation, and turn to thee for grace to use that knowledge for the good of all mankind. Through Jesus Christ our Lord. *Amen.*   [MFP, 275]

Almighty God, Creator of all things, your dominion extends throughout the immensities of space: Guide and guard, we pray, those who seek to probe the mysteries of the universe. Save us all from that arrogance which attributes the achievements of this age to the ability of man alone, and grant that our courses through the sky may lead us to appreciate the majesty of your creation; through Jesus Christ our Lord. *Amen.* [PTL, 54][7]

For those whose work is difficult

Lord, you have taught us that we are members of one another: Hear our prayer for all who do the tedious, dirty, and dangerous work which is necessary to sustain our life; and grant that all who depend upon their service may remember them with thanks; through Jesus Christ our Lord. *Amen.* [PTL, 47][8]

For courts of justice

Almighty God, whose ways are just and whose judgments are true: Guide with your never-failing wisdom the Supreme Court and other courts of justice in our land. Give to our judges and those who assist them, patience, integrity, and compassion; that, remembering that the people they serve are yours, they may discern the truth and impartially administer justice; through Jesus Christ our Lord. *Amen.* [PTL, 42][9]

Almighty God, who sits in the throne judging right: We humbly beseech you to bless the courts of justice and the magistrates in all this land; and give to them the spirit of wisdom and understanding, that they may discern the truth, and impartially administer the law in the fear of you alone; through him who shall come to be our Judge, your Son our Savior Jesus Christ. *Amen.* [821]

For vocation in daily work

Almighty God our heavenly Father, you declare your glory
and show forth your handiwork in the heavens and in the
earth: Deliver us in our various occupations from the service
of self alone, that we may do the work you give us to do in
truth and beauty and for the common good; for the sake of
him who came among us as one who serves, your Son Jesus
Christ our Lord, who lives and reigns with you and the Holy
Spirit, one God, for ever and ever. *Amen.* [261]

For doctors and nurses

Sanctify, O Lord, those whom you have called to the study
and practice of the arts of healing, and to the prevention of
disease and pain. Strengthen them by your life-giving Spirit,
that by their ministries the health of the community may be
promoted and your creation glorified; through Jesus Christ
our Lord. *Amen.* [460]

For fire fighters and police

We beseech thee, Almighty God, to pour thy blessing upon
the fire fighters and the police of our land: strengthen and
preserve them in every danger; that they, who protect our
lives and property while they faithfully perform their duties,
may so serve thee here that they fail not finally to attain thy
heavenly promises. Through Jesus Christ our Lord.
Amen. [MFP, 276]

For nursing homes

O Lord Jesus Christ, who has compassion upon all whom
thou hast made: mercifully behold the nursing homes of our
land, and those who live and work therein (especially
_____). Give them an increase of faith, hope and charity;

give them sure confidence in thy never-failing care and love;
and grant them all things needful, both for this life and that
which is to come. Who with the Father, in the unity of the
Holy Spirit, livest and reignest God, world without end.
Amen.   [MFP, 275]

A farmer's prayer

Almighty and everlasting God, Creator of all things and giver
of all life, let your blessing be upon this (seed, livestock,
plough, forest, _____) and grant that *it* may serve to your
glory and the welfare of your people; through Jesus Christ
our Lord. *Amen.*   [BOOS, 102]

For agriculture

Almighty God, we thank you for making the earth fruitful,
so that it might produce what is needed for life: Bless those
who work in the fields; give us seasonable weather; and
grant that we may all share the fruits of the earth, rejoicing in
your goodness; through Jesus Christ our Lord. *Amen.*   [824]

For the army

O Lord God of Hosts, stretch forth, we pray thee, thine
almighty arm to strengthen and protect the soldiers of our
country. Support them in the day of battle, and in the time of
peace keep them safe from all evil; endue them with courage
and loyalty; and grant that in all things they may serve
without reproach; through Jesus Christ our Lord.
Amen.   [28BCP, 41]

For the aged

Remember, O Lord, we pray, the men and women who reach the summit of their years. Teach them to lay aside former responsibilities without regret and to enjoy new leisure with delight. Keep their minds open and make their hearts young. Sustain them in health, surround them with love, and crown their days with such a living sense of your presence that they may be prepared to see you face to face in your heavenly kingdom; through Jesus Christ our Lord. *Amen.*   [PTL, 59][10]

Look with mercy, O God our Father, on all whose increasing years bring them weakness, distress, or isolation. Provide for them homes of dignity and peace; give them understanding helpers, and the willingness to accept help; and, as their strength diminishes, increase their faith and their assurance of your love. This we ask in the name of Jesus Christ our Lord. *Amen.*   [830]

In time of dearth and famine

O God, heavenly Father, whose gift it is that the rain doth fall, and the earth bring forth her increase; Behold, we beseech thee, the afflictions of thy people; increase the fruits of the earth by thy heavenly benediction; and grant that the scarcity and dearth, which we now most justly suffer for our sins, may, through thy goodness, be mercifully turned into plenty; for the love of Jesus Christ our Lord, to whom, with thee and the Holy Ghost, be all honor and glory, now and for ever. *Amen.*   [28BCP, 40]

For an election

Almighty God, to whom we must account for all our powers and privileges: Guide the people of the United States (*or* of this community) in the election of officials and representatives;

that, by faithful administration and wise laws, the rights of all may be protected and our nation be enabled to fulfill your purposes; through Jesus Christ our Lord. *Amen.*   [822]

O Lord, we beg thee to govern the minds of all who are called at this time to choose faithful persons to serve in the government of this land (*or as need may require*): that they may exercise their choice as in thy sight, for the welfare of all our people; through Jesus Christ our Lord. *Amen.* [MFP, 270]

Almighty God, the fountain of all wisdom, guide and direct, we humbly beseech thee, the minds of all those who are called at this time to exercise the responsible duty of electing fit persons to serve in the government of this nation (*or* of this state *or* city *or* town). Grant that the effect and right issue of their choice may promote thy glory and the welfare of this people; and to all those who shall be elected, give, we pray thee, the spirit of wisdom, courage, sympathy, and true godliness. And this we ask for the sake of our Lord and Savior, Jesus Christ. *Amen.*   [PPB, NO. 72][11]

For Christian citizenship

We beseech thee, O Lord, mercifully to behold the people of this land who are called after thy holy Name; and grant that we may ever walk worthy of our Christian profession. Laying aside our divisions, may we be united in heart and mind to bear the burdens which are laid upon us. Help us to respond to the call of our country according to our several powers; put far from us selfish indifference to the needs of others; and give us grace to fulfill our daily duties with sober diligence. Keep us from all uncharitableness in word or deed; and enable us by patient continuance in well-doing to glorify thy Name; through Jesus Christ our Lord. *Amen.*   [MFP, 271]

For social agencies

Almighty God, whose compassions fail not, and who hast taught us to have compassion upon those in need, prosper, we pray thee the work of our social agencies, and especially, _____ . Stir up the wills of all our people to support them in the relief of want and suffering, and let us not rest until we have provided for the needs of thy children, giving generously as thou hast given to us. *Amen.*   [PPB, NO. 68][12]

For a business or service club

Almighty God, whose great commandment is that we shall love our neighbors as ourselves, and who hast taught us that we should do to others as we would have them do to us, we ask thy blessing upon the work of this club. As our purpose is to help our fellowmen and to promote all that is good in the life of our community, so we pray that thou wilt strengthen our hands in all our undertakings, and that our work may spread the spirit of fellowship and goodwill among all men. *Amen.*   [PPB, NO. 66][12]

For the opening of schools

Bless, we pray thee, O Father, the children and youth of this nation, returning to their schools and colleges. May thy Holy Spirit enlighten their minds, purify their vision, and strengthen their wills; that being taught of thee they may learn to follow in the steps of him who grew in wisdom and stature, and in favor with God and man; through Jesus Christ our Lord. *Amen.*   [PPB, NO. 122][13]

For social service

Heavenly Father, whose blessed Son came not to be served but to serve: Bless all who, following in his steps, give themselves to the service of others; that with wisdom, patience, and courage, they may minister in his Name to the suffering, the friendless, and the needy; for the love of him who laid down his life for us, your Son our Savior Jesus Christ, who lives and reigns with you and the Holy Spirit, one God, for ever and ever. *Amen.*   [260]

For stewardship of creation

O merciful Creator, your hand is open wide to satisfy the needs of every living creature: Make us always thankful for your loving providence; and grant that we, remembering the account that we must one day give, may be faithful stewards of your good gifts; through Jesus Christ our Lord, who with you and the Holy Spirit lives and reigns, one God, for ever and ever. *Amen.*   [259]

For those who suffer for sake of conscience

O God our Father, whose Son forgave his enemies while he was suffering shame and death: Strengthen those who suffer for the sake of conscience; when they are accused, save them from speaking in hate; when they are rejected, save them from bitterness; when they are imprisoned, save them from despair; and to us your servants, give grace to respect their witness and to discern the truth, that our society may be cleansed and strengthened. This we ask for the sake of Jesus Christ, our merciful and righteous Judge. *Amen.*   [823]

At a graduation

O God, we ask thy blessing upon this school (college): its teachers, students, administrators and benefactors; prosper its life in this community, and grant to its graduates a readiness to support the right as they see the right, and the satisfaction of usefulness in the world which thou hast made; through Jesus Christ our Lord. *Amen.*   [PPB, NO. 88][14]

For college work

Guide, we beseech thee, Almighty God, our sons and daughters in the schools and colleges of this land. Protect them in danger, enlighten them in study, kindle them in imagination, confirm them in usefulness. Bless with wisdom and honesty those who minister to them in their needs, both intellectual and spiritual, and bring them close to thee, who art the beginning and ending of all truth; through Jesus Christ our Lord. *Amen.*   [PPB, NO. 127][14]

For fellowship among the nations

Almighty God, who art the Father of all men upon the earth, most heartily we pray that thou wilt keep thy children from cruelties of war, and lead the nations in the way of peace. Teach us to put away all bitterness and misunderstanding, both in church and state; that we, with all the brethren of the Son of Man, may draw together as one comity of peoples, and dwell evermore in the fellowship of that Prince of Peace, who liveth and reigneth with thee in the unity of the Holy Spirit, now and ever. *Amen.*   [PPB, NO. 529][15]

Atomic power

Almighty and merciful God, without whom all things hasten to destruction and fall into nothingness; look, we beseech thee, upon thy family of nations and men, to which thou hast committed power in trust for their mutual health and comfort. Save us and help us, O Lord, lest we abuse thy gift and make it our misery and ruin; draw all men unto thee in

thy kingdom of righteousness and truth; uproot our enmities, heal our divisions, cast out our fears; and renew our faith in thine unchanging purpose of goodwill and peace on earth; for the love of Jesus Christ our Lord. *Amen.*
[PPB, NO. 536][16]

A prayer of nations

Almighty God, supreme Governor of all men: Incline thine ear, we beseech thee, to the prayer of nations, and so overrule the imperfect counsel of men, and set straight the things they cannot govern, that we may walk in the paths of obedience to places of vision, and to thoughts that purge and make us wise; through Jesus Christ our Lord. *Amen.*
[PPB, NO. 532][13]

II
Personal and Corporate Concerns

Personal and Corporate Concerns

For the answering of prayer

Almighty God, who hast promised to hear the petitions of
those who ask in thy Son's Name: We beseech thee mercifully
to incline thine ear to us who have now made our prayers
and supplications unto thee; and grant that those things
which we have faithfully asked according to thy will, may
effectually be obtained, to the relief of our necessity, and to
the setting forth of thy glory; through Jesus Christ our Lord.
Amen. [834]

For an increased knowledge of Christ

Almighty God, whom truly to know is everlasting life: Grant
us so perfectly to know your Son Jesus Christ to be the way,
the truth, and the life, that we may steadfastly follow his
steps in the way that leads to eternal life; through Jesus
Christ your Son our Lord, who lives and reigns with you, in
the unity of the Holy Spirit, one God, for ever and ever.
Amen. [225]

For Christ's compassion

Lord Jesus Christ, Son of the living God, we pray you to set
your passion, cross, and death between your judgment and
our souls, now and in the hour of our death. Give mercy and
grace to the living; pardon and rest to the dead; to your holy

Church peace and concord; and to us sinners everlasting life and glory; for with the Father and Holy Spirit you live and reign, one God, now and for ever. *Amen.*   [282]

For self-acceptance

God, give us the serenity to accept the things we cannot change, the courage to change the things we can, and the wisdom to distinguish the one from the other. *Amen.* [PTL, 69][17]

For following Christ's example

Almighty God, you have given your only Son to be for us a sacrifice for sin, and also an example of godly life: Give us grace to receive thankfully the fruits of his redeeming work, and to follow daily in the blessed steps of his most holy life; through Jesus Christ your Son our Lord, who lives and reigns with you and the Holy Spirit, one God, now and for ever. *Amen.*   [232]

For sharing in Christ's life

O God, who wonderfully created, and yet more wonderfully restored, the dignity of human nature: Grant that we may share the divine life of him who humbled himself to share our humanity, your Son Jesus Christ; who lives and reigns with you, in the unity of the Holy Spirit, one God, for ever and ever. *Amen.*   [214]

For abiding in Christ's presence

O God, who by the glorious resurrection of your Son Jesus Christ destroyed death and brought life and immortality to light: Grant that we, who have been raised with him, may abide in his presence and rejoice in the hope of eternal glory; through Jesus Christ our Lord, to whom, with you and the Holy Spirit, be dominion and praise for ever and ever. *Amen.* [223]

For faith to perceive Christ's presence

Almighty God, whose blessed Son our Savior Jesus Christ ascended far above all heavens that he might fill all things: Mercifully give us faith to perceive that, according to his promise, he abides with his Church on earth, even to the end of the ages; through Jesus Christ our Lord, who lives and reigns with you and the Holy Spirit, one God, in glory everlasting. *Amen.* [226]

For clean thoughts

Almighty God, to you all hearts are open, all desires known, and from you no secrets are hid: Cleanse the thoughts of our hearts by the inspiration of your Holy Spirit, that we may perfectly love you, and worthily magnify your holy Name; through Christ our Lord. *Amen.* [355]

For grace in keeping the commandments

O God, the strength of all who put their trust in you: Mercifully accept our prayers; and because in our weakness we can do nothing good without you, give us the help of your grace, that in keeping your commandments we may please you both in will and deed; through Jesus Christ our Lord, who lives and reigns with you and the Holy Spirit, one God, for ever and ever. *Amen.* [216]

For courage to carry our cross

Almighty God, whose Son our Savior Jesus Christ was lifted high upon the cross that he might draw the whole world to himself: Mercifully grant that we, who glory in the mystery of our redemption, may have grace to take up our cross and follow him; who lives and reigns with you and the Holy Spirit, one God, in glory everlasting. *Amen.*   [244]

In times of crisis

O God, the protector of all who trust in you, without whom nothing is strong, nothing is holy: Increase and multiply upon us your mercy; that, with you as our ruler and guide, we may so pass through things temporal, that we lose not the things eternal; through Jesus Christ our Lord, who lives and reigns with you and the Holy Spirit, one God, for ever and ever. *Amen.*   [231]

For God's leading

O God, by the leading of a star you manifested your only Son to the peoples of the earth: Lead us, who know you now by faith, to your presence, where we may see your glory face to face; through Jesus Christ our Lord, who lives and reigns with you and the Holy Spirit, one God, now and for ever. *Amen.*   [214]

For the abundance of God's mercy

Almighty and everlasting God, you are always more ready to hear than we to pray, and to give more than we either desire or deserve: Pour upon us the abundance of your mercy, forgiving us those things of which our conscience is afraid, and giving us those good things for which we are not worthy to ask, except through the merits and mediation of Jesus Christ our Savior; who lives and reigns with you and the Holy Spirit, one God, for ever and ever. *Amen.*   [234]

For God's protection

Almighty God, you know that we have no power in ourselves to help ourselves: Keep us both outwardly in our bodies and inwardly in our souls, that we may be defended from all adversities which may happen to the body, and from all evil thoughts which may assault and hurt the soul; through Jesus Christ our Lord, who lives and reigns with you and the Holy Spirit, one God, for ever and ever. *Amen.*   [218]

For being good evangelists

Lord Jesus Christ, you stretched out your arms of love on the hard wood of the cross that everyone might come within the reach of your saving embrace: So clothe us in your Spirit that we, reaching forth our hands in love, may bring those who do not know you to the knowledge and love of you; for the honor of your Name. *Amen.*   [101]

For steadfast faith

Almighty God, you have revealed to your Church your eternal Being of glorious majesty and perfect love as one God in Trinity of Persons: Give us grace to continue steadfast in the confession of this faith, and constant in our worship of you, Father, Son, and Holy Spirit; for you live and reign, one God, now and for ever. *Amen.*   [251]

For the increase of faith, hope and love

Almighty and everlasting God, increase in us the gifts of
faith, hope, and charity; and, that we may obtain what you
promise, make us love what you command; through Jesus
Christ our Lord, who lives and reigns with you and the Holy
Spirit, one God, for ever and ever. *Amen.*   [235]

For faithful service

Almighty and merciful God, it is only by your gift that your
faithful people offer you true and laudable service: Grant
that we may run without stumbling to obtain your heavenly
promises; through Jesus Christ our Lord, who lives and
reigns with you and the Holy Spirit, one God, now and for
ever. *Amen.*   [235]

For the followers of Christ

Almighty God, we pray you graciously to behold this your
family, for whom our Lord Jesus Christ was willing to be
betrayed, and given into the hands of sinners, and to suffer
death upon the cross; who now lives and reigns with you and
the Holy Spirit, one God, for ever and ever. *Amen.*   [276]

For a daily death to sin

Almighty God, who for our redemption gave your
only-begotten Son to the death of the cross, and by his
glorious resurrection delivered us from the power of our
enemy: Grant us so to die daily to sin, that we may evermore
live with him in the joy of his resurrection; through Jesus
Christ your Son our Lord, who lives and reigns with you and
the Holy Spirit, one God, now and for ever. *Amen.*   [295]

For grace in daily living

O God, you declare your almighty power chiefly in showing mercy and pity: Grant us the fullness of your grace, that we, running to obtain your promises, may become partakers of your heavenly treasure; through Jesus Christ our Lord, who lives and reigns with you and the Holy Spirit, one God, for ever and ever. *Amen.* [234]

In our daily work

Heavenly Father, in you we live and move and have our being: We humbly pray you so to guide and govern us by your Holy Spirit, that in all the cares and occupations of our life we may not forget you, but may remember that we are ever walking in your sight; through Jesus Christ our Lord. *Amen.* [100]

For dedication to God

Stir up your power, O Lord, and with great might come among us; and, because we are sorely hindered by our sins, let your bountiful grace and mercy speedily help and deliver us; through Jesus Christ our Lord, to whom, with you and the Holy Spirit, be honor and glory, now and for ever. *Amen.* [212]

In times of anxiety

Most loving Father, whose will it is for us to give thanks for all things, to fear nothing but the loss of you, and to cast all our care on you who care for us: Preserve us from faithless fears and worldly anxieties, that no clouds of this mortal life may hide from us the light of that love which is immortal,

and which you have manifested to us in your Son Jesus
Christ our Lord; who lives and reigns with you, in the unity
of the Holy Spirit, one God, now and for ever. *Amen.*   [216]

For following the apostles and prophets

Almighty God, you have built your Church upon the
foundation of the apostles and prophets, Jesus Christ himself
being the chief cornerstone: Grant us so to be joined together
in unity of spirit by their teaching, that we may be made a
holy temple acceptable to you; through Jesus Christ our
Lord, who lives and reigns with you and the Holy Spirit, one
God, for ever and ever. *Amen.*   [230]

For the attainment of heaven

Grant, we pray, Almighty God, that as we believe your
only-begotten Son our Lord Jesus Christ to have ascended
into heaven, so we may also in heart and mind there ascend,
and with him continually dwell; who lives and reigns with
you and the Holy Spirit, one God, for ever and ever.
Amen.   [226]

For keeping the baptismal covenant

Father in heaven, who at the baptism of Jesus in the River
Jordan proclaimed him your beloved Son and anointed him
with the Holy Spirit: Grant that all who are baptized into his
Name may keep the covenant they have made, and boldly
confess him as Lord and Savior; who with you and the Holy
Spirit lives and reigns, one God, in glory everlasting.
Amen.   [214]

For harmony with God and man

O God, you have taught us to keep all your commandments by loving you and our neighbor: Grant us the grace of your Holy Spirit, that we may be devoted to you with our whole heart, and united to one another with pure affection; through Jesus Christ our Lord, who lives and reigns with you and the Holy Spirit, one God, for ever and ever. *Amen.* [230]

For the hastening of God's kingdom

Hasten, O Father, the coming of your kingdom; and grant that we your servants, who now live by faith, may with joy behold your Son at his coming in glorious majesty; even Jesus Christ, our only Mediator and Advocate. *Amen.* [395]

For help of holy angels

Everlasting God, you have ordained and constituted in a wonderful order the ministries of angels and mortals: Mercifully grant that, as your holy angels always serve and worship you in heaven, so by your appointment they may help and defend us here on earth; through Jesus Christ our Lord, who lives and reigns with you and the Holy Spirit, one God, for ever and ever. *Amen.* [251]

For direction of the Holy Spirit

O God, because without you we are not able to please you, mercifully grant that your Holy Spirit may in all things direct and rule our hearts; through Jesus Christ our Lord, who lives and reigns with you and the Holy Spirit, one God, now and for ever. *Amen.* [233]

For all people

O God, you have made of one blood all the peoples of the earth, and sent your blessed Son to preach peace to those who are far off and to those who are near: Grant that people everywhere may seek after you and find you; bring the nations into your fold; pour out your Spirit upon all flesh; and hasten the coming of your kingdom; through Jesus Christ our Lord. *Amen.*   [100]

For aid against perils

Almighty and merciful God, in your goodness keep us, we pray, from all things that may hurt us, that we, being ready both in mind and body, may accomplish with free hearts those things which belong to your purpose; through Jesus Christ our Lord, who lives and reigns with you and the Holy Spirit, one God, now and for ever. *Amen.*   [228]

In times of perplexity

O God, from whom all good proceeds: Grant that by your inspiration we may think those things that are right, and by your merciful guiding may do them; through Jesus Christ our Lord, who lives and reigns with you and the Holy Spirit, one God, for ever and ever. *Amen.*   [229]

For grace to heed the prophets

Merciful God, who sent your messengers the prophets to preach repentance and prepare the way for our salvation: Give us grace to heed their warnings and forsake our sins, that we may greet with you the coming of Jesus Christ our Redeemer; who lives and reigns with you and the Holy Spirit, one God, now and for ever. *Amen.*   [211]

For protection in life

Assist us mercifully, O Lord, in these our supplications and prayers, and dispose the way of your servants towards the attainment of everlasting salvation; that, among all the changes and chances of this mortal life, they may ever be defended by your gracious and ready help; through Jesus Christ our Lord. *Amen.* [832]

For purification of conscience

Purify our conscience, Almighty God, by your daily visitation, that your Son Jesus Christ, at his coming, may find in us a mansion prepared for himself; who lives and reigns with you, in the unity of the Holy Spirit, one God, now and for ever. *Amen.* [212]

For purity of living

O God, whose blessed Son came into the world that he might destroy the works of the devil and make us children of God and heirs of eternal life: Grant that, having this hope, we may purify ourselves as he is pure; that, when he comes again with power and great glory, we may be made like him in his eternal and glorious kingdom; where he lives and reigns with you and the Holy Spirit, one God, for ever and ever. *Amen.* [236]

For quiet confidence

O God of peace, who has taught us that in returning and rest we shall be saved, in quietness and in confidence shall be our strength: By the might of your Spirit lift us, we pray you, to your presence, where we may be still and know that you are God; through Jesus Christ our Lord. *Amen.* [832]

For a despondent person

Comfort, we beseech thee, most gracious God, this thy
servant, cast down and faint of heart amidst the sorrows and
difficulties of the world; and grant that, by the power of thy
Holy Spirit, *he* may be enabled to go upon *his* way rejoicing,
and give thee continual thanks for thy sustaining providence;
through Jesus Christ our Lord. *Amen.*   [MFP, 43]

For grace to live aright

O heavenly Father, who in thy son Jesus Christ, hast given us
a true faith, and a sure hope: help us, we pray thee, to live as
those who believe in the Communion of Saints, the
forgiveness of sins, and the Resurrection to life everlasting,
and strengthen this faith and hope in us all the days of our
life, through the love of thy Son, Jesus Christ our Savior.
Amen.   [MFP, 120]

For strength in bearing our cross

O God, who before the passion of your only-begotten Son
revealed his glory upon the holy mountain: Grant to us that
we, beholding by faith the light of his countenance, may be
strengthened to bear our cross, and be changed into his
likeness from glory to glory; through Jesus Christ our Lord,
who lives and reigns with you and the Holy Spirit, one God,
for ever and ever. *Amen.*   [217]

In times of stress

O God, who on the holy mount revealed to chosen witnesses
your well-beloved Son, wonderfully transfigured, in raiment
white and glistening: Mercifully grant that we, being
delivered from the disquietude of this world, may by faith

behold the King in his beauty; who with you, O Father, and you, O Holy Spirit, lives and reigns, one God, for ever and ever. *Amen.* [243]

In honoring the Virgin Mary

Father in heaven, by your grace the virgin mother of your incarnate Son was blessed in bearing him, but still more blessed in keeping your word: Grant us who honor the exaltation of her lowliness to follow the example of her devotion to your will; through Jesus Christ our Lord, who lives and reigns with you and the Holy Spirit, one God, for ever and ever. *Amen.* [240]

In walking the way of the cross

Almighty God, whose most dear Son went not up to joy but first he suffered pain, and entered not into glory before he was crucified: Mercifully grant that we, walking in the way of the cross, may find it none other than the way of life and peace; through Jesus Christ your Son our Lord, who lives and reigns with you and the Holy Spirit, one God, for ever and ever. *Amen.* [220]

For the water of life

O God, you have created all things by the power of your Word, and you renew the earth by your Spirit: Give now the water of life to those who thirst for you, that they may bring forth abundant fruit in your glorious kingdom; through Jesus Christ our Lord. *Amen.* [290]

For worthiness in our calling

Remember, O Lord, what you have wrought in us and not what we deserve; and, as you have called us to your service, make us worthy of our calling; through Jesus Christ our Lord, who lives and reigns with you and the Holy Spirit, one God, now and for ever. *Amen.*   [228]

For transformation of character

Almighty and everlasting God, you hate nothing you have made and forgive the sins of all who are penitent: Create and make in us new and contrite hearts, that we, worthily lamenting our sins and acknowledging our wretchedness, may obtain of you, the God of all mercy, perfect remission and forgiveness; through Jesus Christ our Lord, who lives and reigns with you and the Holy Spirit, one God, for ever and ever. *Amen.*   [217]

In times of trouble

We humbly beseech you, O Father, mercifully to look upon our infirmities; and for the glory of your Name, turn from us all those evils that we most justly have deserved; and grant that in all our troubles we may put our whole trust and confidence in your mercy, and evermore serve you in holiness and pureness of living, to your honor and glory; through our only Mediator and Advocate, Jesus Christ our Lord. *Amen.*   [155]

For trust in God

Grant us, O Lord, to trust in you with all our hearts; for, as you always resist the proud who confide in their own strength, so you never forsake those who make their boast of

your mercy; through Jesus Christ our Lord, who lives and
reigns with you and the Holy Spirit, one God, now and for
ever. *Amen.* [233]

In times of temptation

Almighty God, whose blessed Son was led by the Spirit
to be tempted by Satan: Come quickly to help us who are
assaulted by many temptations; and, as you know the
weaknesses of each of us, let each one find you mighty to
save; through Jesus Christ your Son our Lord, who lives and
reigns with you and the Holy Spirit, one God, now and for
ever. *Amen.* [218]

For the acceptance of our prayers

O Lord our God, accept the fervent prayers of your people;
in the multitude of your mercies, look with compassion upon
us and all who turn to you for help; for you are gracious, O
lover of souls, and to you we give glory, Father, Son, and
Holy Spirit, now and for ever. *Amen.* [395]

For righteous living

Grant to us, Lord, we pray, the spirit to think and do always
those things that are right, that we, who cannot exist without
you, may by you be enabled to live according to your will;
through Jesus Christ our Lord, who lives and reigns with you
and the Holy Spirit, one God, for ever and ever. *Amen.* [232]

A prayer of self-dedication

Almighty and eternal God, so draw our hearts to you, so
guide our minds, so fill our imaginations, so control our
wills, that we may be wholly yours, utterly dedicated to you;

and then use us, we pray you, as you will, and always to your glory and the welfare of your people; through Jesus Christ our Lord. *Amen.* [832]

In times of shame and loss

O God, by the passion of your blessed Son you made an instrument of shameful death to be for us the means of life: Grant us so to glory in the cross of Christ, that we may gladly suffer shame and loss for the sake of your Son our Savior Jesus Christ; who lives and reigns with you and the Holy Spirit, one God, for ever and ever. *Amen.* [220]

For freedom from sin

Set us free, O God, from the bondage of our sins, and give us the liberty of that abundant life which you have made known to us in your Son our Savior Jesus Christ; who lives and reigns with you, in the unity of the Holy Spirit, one God, now and for ever. *Amen.* [216]

For those fallen into sin

O God, whose glory it is always to have mercy: Be gracious to all who have gone astray from your ways, and bring them again with penitent hearts and steadfast faith to embrace and hold fast the unchangeable truth of your Word, Jesus Christ your Son; who with you and the Holy Spirit lives and reigns, one God, for ever and ever. *Amen.* [218]

For stability in Christ

Almighty God, you alone can bring into order the unruly wills and affections of sinners: Grant your people grace to love what you command and desire what you promise; that

among the swift and varied changes of the world, our hearts
may surely there be fixed where true joys are to be found;
through Jesus Christ our Lord, who lives and reigns with you
and the Holy Spirit, one God, now and for ever.
Amen. [219]

In times of need

O Lord, mercifully receive the prayers of your people who
call upon you, and grant that they may know and understand
what things they ought to do, and also may have grace and
power faithfully to accomplish them; through Jesus Christ
our Lord, who lives and reigns with you and the Holy Spirit,
one God, now and for ever. *Amen.* [231]

For the reborn in Christ

Almighty and everlasting God, who in the Paschal mystery
established the new covenant of reconciliation: Grant that all
who have been reborn into the fellowship of Christ's Body
may show forth in their lives what they profess by their faith;
through Jesus Christ our Lord, who lives and reigns with you
and the Holy Spirit, one God, for ever and ever.
Amen. [223]

For the renewal of life

O God, the King eternal, whose light divides the day from
the night and turns the shadow of death into the morning:
Drive far from us all wrong desires, incline our hearts to keep
your law, and guide our feet into the way of peace; that,
having done your will with cheerfulness during the day, we
may, when night comes, rejoice to give you thanks; through
Jesus Christ our Lord. *Amen.* [99]

For respecting God

O Lord, make us have perpetual love and reverence for your holy Name, for you never fail to help and govern those whom you have set upon the sure foundation of your loving-kindness; through Jesus Christ our Lord, who lives and reigns with you and the Holy Spirit, one God, for ever and ever. *Amen.*   [230]

For the patience and humility of Christ

Almighty and everliving God, in your tender love for the human race you sent your Son our Savior Jesus Christ to take upon him our nature, and to suffer death upon the cross, giving us the example of his great humility: Mercifully grant that we may walk in the way of his suffering, and also share in his resurrection; through Jesus Christ our Lord, who lives and reigns with you and the Holy Spirit, one God, for ever and ever. *Amen.*   [219]

In meditating on the passion

Assist us mercifully with your help, O Lord God of our salvation, that we may enter with joy upon the contemplation of those mighty acts, whereby you have given us life and immortality; through Jesus Christ our Lord. *Amen.*   [270]

For the love of Christ

Eternal Father, you gave to your incarnate Son the holy name of Jesus to be the sign of our salvation: Plant in every heart, we pray, the love of him who is the Savior of the world, our Lord Jesus Christ; who lives and reigns with you and the Holy Spirit, one God, in glory everlasting. *Amen.*   [213]

For the love of God

O God, you have prepared for those who love you such good things as surpass our understanding: Pour into our hearts such love towards you, that we, loving you in all things and above all things, may obtain your promises, which exceed all that we can desire; through Jesus Christ our Lord, who lives and reigns with you and the Holy Spirit, one God, for ever and ever. *Amen.* [225]

For deliverance from malice and wickedness

Almighty Father, who gave your only Son to die for our sins and to rise for our justification: Give us grace so to put away the leaven of malice and wickedness, that we may always serve you in pureness of living and truth; through Jesus Christ your Son our Lord, who lives and reigns with you and the Holy Spirit, one God, now and for ever. *Amen.* [224]

For rejoicing in the inheritance of Israel

O God, whose wonderful deeds of old shine forth even to our own day, you once delivered by the power of your mighty arm your chosen people from slavery under Pharaoh, to be a sign for us of the salvation of all nations by the water of Baptism: Grant that all the peoples of the earth may be numbered among the offspring of Abraham, and rejoice in the inheritance of Israel; through Jesus Christ our Lord. *Amen.* [289]

For inner peace

Almighty and everlasting God, you govern all things both in heaven and on earth: Mercifully hear the supplications of your people, and in our time grant us your peace; through Jesus Christ our Lord, who lives and reigns with you and the Holy Spirit, one God, for ever and ever. *Amen.*   [215]

For the light of Christ

Almighty God, you have poured upon us the new light of your incarnate Word: Grant that this light, enkindled in our hearts, may shine forth in our lives; through Jesus Christ our Lord, who lives and reigns with you, in the unity of the Holy Spirit, one God, now and for ever. *Amen.*   [213]

Preparing for church worship

Almighty God, who after the creation of the world rested from all your works and sanctified a day of rest for all your creatures: Grant that we, putting away all earthly anxieties, may be duly prepared for the service of your sanctuary, and that our rest here upon earth may be a preparation for the eternal rest promised to your people in heaven; through Jesus Christ our Lord. *Amen.*   [99]

For enlightenment of the Holy Spirit

Almighty and most merciful God, grant that by the indwelling of your Holy Spirit we may be enlightened and strengthened for your service; through Jesus Christ our Lord, who lives and reigns with you, in the unity of the Holy Spirit, one God, now and for ever. *Amen.*   [251]

For help of the Holy Spirit

Heavenly Father, send your Holy Spirit into our hearts, to direct and rule us according to your will, to comfort us in all our afflictions, to defend us from all error, and to lead us into all truth; through Jesus Christ our Lord. *Amen.*   [107]

For strength of the Holy Spirit

O God, the King of glory, you have exalted your only Son
Jesus Christ with great triumph to your kingdom in heaven:
Do not leave us comfortless, but send us your Holy Spirit to
strengthen us, and exalt us to that place where our Savior
Christ has gone before; who lives and reigns with you and
the Holy Spirit, one God, in glory everlasting. *Amen.* [226]

For effective Christian witness

Almighty God, whose Son our Savior Jesus Christ is the light
of the world: Grant that your people, illumined by your
Word and Sacraments, may shine with the radiance of
Christ's glory, that he may be known, worshiped, and obeyed
to the ends of the earth; through Jesus Christ our Lord, who
with you and the Holy Spirit lives and reigns, one God, now
and for ever. *Amen.* [215]

For the perception of eternal truths

Grant us, Lord, not to be anxious about earthly things, but
to love things heavenly; and even now, while we are placed
among things that are passing away, to hold fast to those that
shall endure; through Jesus Christ our Lord, who lives and
reigns with you and the Holy Spirit, one God, for ever and
ever. *Amen.* [234]

For the fruit of good works

Lord of all power and might, the author and giver of all good
things: Graft in our hearts the love of your Name; increase in
us true religion; nourish us with all goodness; and bring
forth in us the fruit of good works; through Jesus Christ our
Lord, who lives and reigns with you and the Holy Spirit, one
God for ever and ever. *Amen.* [233]

For grace

Lord, we pray that your grace may always precede and
follow us, that we may continually be given to good works;
through Jesus Christ our Lord, who lives and reigns with you
and the Holy Spirit, one God, now and for ever.
Amen. [234]

For guidance

O God, by whom the meek are guided in judgment, and light
rises up in darkness for the godly; Grant us, in all our doubts
and uncertainties, the grace to ask what you would have us
to do, that the Spirit of wisdom may save us from all false
choices, and that in your light we may see light, and in your
straight path may not stumble; through Jesus Christ our
Lord. *Amen.* [832]

For the bread of life

Gracious Father, whose blessed Son Jesus Christ came down
from heaven to be the true bread which gives life to the
world: Evermore give us this bread, that he may live in us,
and we in him; who lives and reigns with you and the Holy
Spirit, one God, now and for ever. *Amen.* [219]

In studying the Scriptures

Blessed Lord, who caused all holy Scriptures to be written for
our learning: Grant us so to hear them, read, mark, learn,
and inwardly digest them, that we may embrace and ever
hold fast the blessed hope of everlasting life, which you have
given us in our Savior Jesus Christ; who lives and reigns with
you and the Holy Spirit, one God, for ever and ever.
Amen. [236]

Before Communion

We do not presume to come to this thy Table, O merciful Lord, trusting in our own righteousness, but in thy manifold and great mercies. We are not worthy so much as to gather up the crumbs under thy Table. But thou art the same Lord whose property is always to have mercy. Grant us therefore, gracious Lord, so to eat the flesh of they dear Son Jesus Christ, and to drink his blood, that we may evermore dwell in him, and he in us. *Amen.*   [337]

Be present, be present, O Jesus, our great High Priest, as you were present with your disciples, and be known to us in the breaking of bread; who live and reign with the Father and the Holy Spirit, now and for ever. *Amen.*   [834]

For defense against our enemies

O God, the author of peace and lover of concord, to know you is eternal life and to serve you is perfect freedom: Defend us, your humble servants, in all assaults of our enemies; that we, surely trusting in your defense, may not fear the power of any adversaries; through the might of Jesus Christ our Lord. *Amen.*   [99]

General confessions

Almighty God,
Father of our Lord Jesus Christ,
maker of all things, judge of all men:
We acknowledge and bewail our manifold sins
    and wickedness,
which we from time to time most grievously have committed,
by thought, word, and deed, against thy divine Majesty,
provoking most justly thy wrath and indignation against us.

We do earnestly repent,
   and are heartily sorry for these our misdoings;
the remembrance of them is grievous unto us,
the burden of them is intolerable.
Have mercy upon us,
   have mercy upon us, most merciful Father;
for thy Son our Lord Jesus Christ's sake,
forgive us all that is past;
and grant that we may ever hereafter
serve and please thee in newness of life,
to the honor and glory of thy Name;
through Jesus Christ our Lord.
Amen.   [331]

Almighty and most merciful Father,
we have erred and strayed from thy ways like lost sheep,
we have followed too much the devices and desires of our
      own hearts,
we have offended against thy holy laws,
we have left undone those things which we ought to
      have done,
and we have done those things which we ought not to
      have done.
But thou, O Lord, have mercy upon us,
spare thou those who confess their faults,
restore thou those who are penitent,
according to thy promises declared unto mankind
in Christ Jesus our Lord;
and grant, O most merciful Father, for his sake,
that we may hereafter live a godly, righteous, and sober life,
to the glory of thy holy Name.
Amen.   [41]

Most merciful God,
We confess that we have sinned against you
   in thought, word, and deed,

by what we have done,
    and by what we have left undone.
We have not loved you with our whole heart;
    we have not loved our neighbors as ourselves.
We are truly sorry and we humbly repent.
For the sake of your Son Jesus Christ,
have mercy on us and forgive us;
that we may delight in your will,
and walk in your ways,
to the glory of your Name.
Amen.   [79]

Just For Today

Lord, for to-morrow and its needs,
        I do not pray;
Keep me, my God, from stain of sin
        Just for to-day.
Let me both diligently work,
        And duly pray.
Let me be kind in word and deed,
        Just for to-day.
Let me be slow to do my will,
        Prompt to obey;
Help me to sacrifice myself
        Just for to-day.
And if to-day my tide of life
        Should ebb away,
Give me thy Sacraments divine,
        Sweet Lord, to-day.
So for tomorrow and its needs
        I do not pray,
But keep me, guide me, love me, Lord,
        Just for to-day.
Amen.   [SAPB, 17]

In marriage counseling

O God, our Father, who knowest all thy children, help us with thy wisdom to understand ourselves and each other; melt our pride with the warmth of thy redeeming charity and take us back to our days of loving trust, that we may build again in the good companionship of Jesus Christ our Lord. *Amen.* [PPB, NO. 116]¹⁴

For direction in all endeavors

Direct us, O Lord, in all our doings with your most gracious favor, and further us with your continual help; that in all our works begun, continued, and ended in you, we may glorify your holy Name, and finally, by your mercy, obtain everlasting life; through Jesus Christ our Lord. *Amen.* [832]

For recognizing Christ's voice

O God, whose Son Jesus is the good shepherd of your people: Grant that when we hear his voice we may know him who calls us each by name, and follow where he leads; who, with you and the Holy Spirit, lives and reigns, one God, for ever and ever. *Amen.* [225]

For insight into Christ's work

O God, whose blessed Son made himself known to his disciples in the breaking of bread: Open the eyes of our faith, that we may behold him in all his redeeming work; who lives and reigns with you, in the unity of the Holy Spirit, one God, now and for ever. *Amen.* [224]

For divine providence

O God, your never-failing providence sets in order all things
both in heaven and earth: Put away from us, we entreat you,
all hurtful things, and give us those things which are
profitable for us; through Jesus Christ our Lord, who lives
and reigns with you and the Holy Spirit, one God, for ever
and ever. *Amen.* [229]

For being kept in eternal life

May Almighty God, the Father of our Lord Jesus Christ, who
has given us a new birth by water and the Holy Spirit, and
bestowed upon us the forgiveness of sins, keep us in eternal
life by his grace, in Christ Jesus our Lord. *Amen.* [294]

For the gift of love

O Lord, you have taught us that without love whatever we
do is worth nothing: Send your Holy Spirit and pour into our
hearts your greatest gift, which is love, the true bond of peace
and of all virtue, without which whoever lives is accounted
dead before you. Grant this for the sake of your only Son
Jesus Christ, who lives and reigns with you and the Holy
Spirit, one God, now and for ever. *Amen.* [216]

For knowledge of God's creation

Almighty and everlasting God, you made the universe with
all its marvelous order, its atoms, worlds, and galaxies, and
the infinite complexity of living creatures: Grant that, as we
probe the mysteries of your creation, we may come to know
you more truly, and more surely fulfill our role in your
eternal purpose; in the name of Jesus Christ our Lord.
Amen. [827]

For the right use of God's gifts

Almighty God, whose loving hand has given us all that we
possess: Grant us grace that we may honor you with our
substance, and, remembering the account which we must one
day give, may be faithful stewards of your bounty, through
Jesus Christ our Lord. *Amen.*   [827]

For vocation in daily work

Almighty God, you give us new life, new hope, and new
opportunities with each returning day: Help us to use these
blessings to the best of our capacity in doing the work which
we have to do; devoting ourselves wholly to your service,
and putting our selfish interests aside to seek the welfare of
our fellow men; for the sake of him who came among us as
one who serves, your Son Jesus Christ our Lord.
Amen.   [PTL, 46][9]

For power to serve and praise God

O God, you have called your people to your service from age
to age. Do not give us over to death, but raise us up to serve
you, to praise you, and to glorify your holy Name; through
Jesus Christ our Lord. *Amen.*   [BOOS, 107]

For living in God's presence

In your wisdom, O Lord our God, you have made all things,
and have allotted to each of us the days of our life: Grant
that we may live in your presence, be guided by your Holy
Spirit, and offer all our works to your honor and glory;
through Jesus Christ our Lord. *Amen.*   [BOOS, 41]

For self-mastery

O Lord, help us to be masters of ourselves that we may be the servants of others; through Jesus Christ our Lord and Master. *Amen.* [PTL, 69][18]

For obeying God's voice

Almighty and everliving God, you have made all things in your wisdom and established the boundaries of life and death: Grant that we may obey your voice in this world, and in the world to come may enjoy that rest and peace which you have appointed for your people; through Jesus Christ who is Resurrection and Life, and who lives and reigns for ever and ever. *Amen.* [BOOS, 106]

For renewal by the Holy Spirit

Almighty and merciful God, through your well beloved Son Jesus Christ, the King of kings and Lord of lords, you have willed to make all things new: Grant that we may be renewed by your Holy Spirit, and may come at last to that heavenly country where your people hunger and thirst no more, and the tears are wiped away from every eye; through Jesus Christ our Lord. *Amen.* [BOOS, 43]

For a right attitude toward work

O God, as your Son, Jesus Christ, was obedient to his knowledge of your purposes for him, help us to understand and obey your purposes for us, and to discover the work we are best fitted to do. And as he steadfastly rejected the temptation to use unworthy means, teach us also to accept the discipline necessary to master our work, and to work for the ends you desire, to the honor of your holy Name. *Amen.* [PTL, 51][19]

A prayer of universal petition

O MY GOD, I BELIEVE IN THEE; do thou strengthen my faith.
All my hopes are in thee; do thou secure them. I love thee
with my whole heart; teach me to love thee daily more and
more. I am sorry that I have offended thee; do thou increase
my sorrow.

I ADORE THEE AS MY FIRST BEGINNING; I aspire after thee as
my last end; I give thee thanks as my constant benefactor;
I call upon thee as my sovereign Protector.

VOUCHSAFE, O MY GOD, to conduct me by thy wisdom, to
restrain me by thy justice, to comfort me by thy mercy, to
defend me by thy power.

TO THEE I DESIRE TO CONSECRATE all my thoughts, words,
actions, and sufferings; that henceforward I may think of
thee, speak of thee, constantly refer all my actions to thy
greater glory, and suffer willingly whatever thou shalt allow
me to suffer.

LORD, I DESIRE that in all things thy will may be done,
because it is thy will, in the manner thou willest, and as long
as thou willest.

I BEG OF THEE TO ENLIGHTEN my understanding, to inflame
my will, to purify my body, and to sanctify my soul.

GRANT THAT I may not be lifted up with pride, moved by
flattery, deceived by the world, or duped by the devil.

GIVE ME GRACE to purify my memory, to bridle my tongue, to
restrain my eyes, and to mortify my senses.

GIVE ME STRENGTH, O MY GOD, to atone for my sins, to
overcome my temptations, to subdue my passions, and to
acquire the virtues proper to my state in life.

FILL MY HEART with tender affection for thy goodness,
hatred for my faults, love for my neighbor, and contempt
of the world.

LET ME ALWAYS REMEMBER to be submissive to authority, faithful to my friends, and charitable to my enemies.

GRANT, O LORD, that I may remember thy rule and example, by loving my enemies, bearing with injuries, doing good to them that persecute me, and praying for them that slander or ill-use me.

ASSIST ME TO OVERCOME sensuality by mortification, avarice by alms-deeds, anger by meekness, and lukewarmness by devotion.

O MY GOD, make me prudent in my undertakings, courageous in dangers, patient in afflictions, and humble in prosperity.

GRANT THAT I MAY BE ever attentive at my prayers, temperate at my meals, diligent in my employments, and constant in my good resolutions.

LET my conscience be ever upright and pure, my exterior modest, my conversation edifying, and my life according to rule.

ASSIST ME, that I may continually labor to overcome my fallen nature, to correspond with thy grace, to keep all thy commandments, and to work out my salvation.

HELP ME TO OBTAIN HOLINESS OF LIFE by a sincere confession of my sins, by a devout reception of the Body and Blood of Christ, by a continual recollection of mind, and by a pure intention of heart.

SHOW TO ME, O MY GOD, the nothingness of this world, the greatness of heaven, the shortness of time, and the length of eternity.

GRANT that I may prepare for death, that I may fear thy judgments, that I may escape hell, and in the end obtain the joy of heaven. For Jesus' sake.

Amen. [SAPB, 31]

A prayer for contrition

O blessed Jesus, look upon me with those eyes with which thou didst look upon Magdalene at the feast, Peter in the hall, the thief upon the cross: that, with the thief, I may entreat thee humbly. Remember me, Lord, in thy kingdom; that, with Peter, I may bitterly weep; that, with Magdalene, I may hear thee say, Thy sins be forgiven thee. *Amen.* [SAPB, 29]

A prayer of union with Jesus

Christ within me;
>   Christ above me;
Christ below me;
>   Christ before me;
Christ behind me;
>   Christ on my right;
Christ on my left;
>   Christ all about me

To guide, and direct me,
That each meeting will be,
Each work undertaken
By, with, and in him
>   Performed to his Glory.

Amen. [SAPB, 30]

For defense against Satan and all evil

O most merciful and mighty God, your son Jesus Christ was born of the Blessed Virgin Mary to bring us salvation and to establish your kingdom on earth: Grant that Michael and all your angels may defend your people against Satan and every evil foe, and that at the last we may come to that heavenly country where your saints for ever sing your praise; through Jesus Christ our Lord. *Amen.* [BOOS, 108]

For grace of an abounding gratitude

We beseech thee, loving Father, to pour into our hearts the grace of an abounding gratitude; that we may ever praise and glorify thee for the goodness and mercy that have followed us all the days of our life. Through Christ our Lord. *Amen.*   [SAPB, 54]

An oblation of self

Accept, O Lord, my entire liberty, my memory, my understanding, and my will. All that I am and have thou hast given to me; and I give all back to thee to be disposed of according to thy good pleasure. Give me only the comfort of thy presence and the joy of thy love; with these I shall be more than rich and shall desire nothing more. *Amen.*   [SAPB, 107]

An act of desire

O most dear Lord Jesus Christ, graciously fill me with true, calm, holiest charity, that I may ever hunger after thee the Bread of Angels, the refreshment of holy souls. Grant that I may ever long to feed upon thee, and that my inmost soul may be filled with the sweetness of thy savor. Grant that my soul may ever thirst for thee, the fountain of life, fountain of wisdom and knowledge, the fountain of eternal light, the torrent of pleasure, and the richness of the house of God. *Amen.*   [SAPB, 148]

For light and guidance

O most blessed Light and Lamp of Souls, who dwellest in the light that no man can approach, and who lighteth every man that cometh into the world: send forth thy light from the everlasting hills that I may see my whole self truly in thy light.

Let me not shrink from seeing anything in me now, that so I may be purified to see thy face with joy hereafter; who livest and reignest, world without end. *Amen.*   [SAPB, 150]

For faith and love among Christians

O God, you have united diverse peoples in the confession of your Name: Grant that all who have been born again in the font of Baptism may also be united in faith and love; through Jesus Christ our Lord, who lives and reigns with you and the Holy Spirit, one God, for ever and ever. *Amen.*   [LFF, 57]

For heavenly gifts

O Lord, you have saved us through the Paschal mystery of Christ: Continue to support your people with heavenly gifts, that we may attain true liberty, and enjoy the happiness of heaven which we have begun to taste on earth; through Jesus Christ our Lord, who lives and reigns with you and the Holy Spirit, one God, for ever and ever. *Amen.*   [LFF, 59]

For God's blessing on new Christians

O God, by the abundance of your grace you unfailingly increase the number of your children: Look with favor upon those whom you have chosen to be members of your Church, that, having been born again in Baptism, they may be granted a glorious resurrection; through Jesus Christ your Son our Lord, who lives and reigns with you and the Holy Spirit, one God, now and for ever. *Amen.*   [LFF, 60]

For the joy of God's kingdom

Almighty and everlasting God, you have given your Church the great joy of the resurrection of Jesus Christ: Give us also the greater joy of the kingdom of your elect, when the flock of your Son will share in the final victory of its Shepherd, Jesus Christ our Lord; who lives and reigns with you and the Holy Spirit, one God, now and for ever. *Amen.*   [LFF, 61]

For strength to persevere in faith

Lord God Almighty, for no merit on our part you have brought us out of death into life, out of sorrow into joy: Put no end to your gifts, fulfill your marvelous acts in us, and grant to us who have been justified by faith the strength to persevere in that faith; through Jesus Christ our Lord, who lives and reigns with you and the Holy Spirit, one God, for ever and ever. *Amen.*   [LFF, 62]

For the transformation of our lives

Grant, Almighty God, that the commemoration of our Lord's death and resurrection may continually transform our lives and be manifested in our deeds; through Jesus Christ our Lord, who lives and reigns with you and the Holy Spirit, one God, for ever and ever. *Amen.*   [LFF, 63]

For perceiving Christ's presence among us

Hear our prayers, O Lord, and, as we confess that Christ, the Savior of the world, lives with you in glory, grant that, as he himself has promised, we may perceive him present among us also, to the end of the ages; who lives and reigns with you and the Holy Spirit, one God, for ever and ever. *Amen.*   [LFF, 64]

For newness of life

O Lord, you have given us the grace to know the resurrection of your Son: Grant that the Holy Spirit, by his love, may raise us to newness of life; through Jesus Christ our Lord, who lives and reigns with you and the Holy Spirit, one God, for ever and ever. *Amen.*   [LFF, 64]

For being clothed in immortality

O God, by the resurrection of your Son you have given us a new birth into eternal life: Lift our hearts to our Savior, who is seated at your right hand, so that, when he comes again, we who have been reborn in Baptism may be clothed in a glorious immortality; through Jesus Christ our Lord, who lives and reigns with you and the Holy Spirit, one God, for ever and ever. *Amen.*   [LFF, 65]

For diligent dedication to God's service

O God, by the glorification of Jesus Christ and the coming of the Holy Spirit you have opened for us the gates of your kingdom: Grant that we, who have received such great gifts, may dedicate ourselves more diligently to your service, and live more fully the riches of our faith; through Jesus Christ our Lord, who lives and reigns with you and the Holy Spirit, one God, for ever and ever. *Amen.*   [LFF, 66]

For the gifts of the Holy Spirit

O Lord, when your Son ascended into heaven he sent down upon the Apostles the Holy Spirit, as he had promised, that they might comprehend the mysteries of the kingdom: Distribute among us also, we pray, the gifts of the selfsame Spirit; through Jesus Christ our Lord, who lives and reigns with you and the Holy Spirit, one God, for ever and ever. *Amen.*   [LFF, 66]

For strength against Satan

O God, through your Son you have taught us to be watchful, and to await the sudden day of judgment: Strengthen us against Satan and his forces of wickedness, the evil powers of this world, and the sinful desires within us; and grant that, having served you all the days of our life, we may finally come to the dwelling place your Son has prepared for us; who lives and reigns for ever and ever. *Amen.* [BOOS, 43]

For today

O God, give me strength to live another day. Let me not turn coward before its difficulties or prove recreant to its duties. Let me not lose faith in my fellow men. Keep me sweet and sound of heart, in spite of ingratitude, treachery, or meanness. Preserve me from minding little stings or giving them. Help me to keep my heart clean, and to live so honestly and fearlessly that no outward failure can dishearten me or take away the joy of conscious integrity. Open wide the eyes of my soul that I may see good in all things. Grant me this day some new vision of thy truth, inspire me with the spirit of joy and gladness, and make me the cup of strength to suffering souls; in the name of the strong Deliverer, our only Lord and Savior, Jesus Christ. *Amen.* [PPB, NO. 12][15]

For those who have not found love

O God of Love, who art in all places and times, pour thy spirit of healing and comfort upon every lonely heart. Have pity upon those who are bereft of human love, and on those to whom it has never come. Be unto them a strong consolation, and in the end give them fullness of joy; for the sake of Jesus Christ our Lord. *Amen.* [PPB, NO. 173][20]

For sleep

O heavenly Father, you give your children sleep for the refreshing of soul and body: Grant me this gift, I pray; keep me in that perfect peace which you have promised to those whose minds are fixed on you; and give me such a sense of your presence, that in the hours of silence I may enjoy the blessed assurance of your love; through Jesus Christ our Savior. *Amen.*   [461]

O Holy Jesus, who had no place to lay thy head, watch with me in the night hours, I beseech thee; calm my fears and relieve my anxieties with thy blessed gift of sleep; give me thy peace and grant that I may wake up refreshed for thy service; who with the Father and the Holy Spirit rulest all things. *Amen.*   [PPB, NO. 175][14]

For one awaiting trial

O God, whose property is always to have mercy when we are hard-hearted, and to forgive when we deserve punishment, look with compassion on this thy *son* in *his* time of trouble; restore the guilty, shield and sustain the innocent, walk with those who are appointed to die. Bless those we love and who love us, give us readiness for repentance and, if it be thy will, time to serve thee in newness of life; through Jesus Christ our Lord. *Amen.*   [PPB, NO. 90][14]

For a blessing on new enterprises

Lord, we desire to place ourselves and what we are about to undertake in thy hands. Guide, direct, and prosper us, we beseech thee; and if thou seest that this undertaking will be for thy glory, grant us good success. Make us and those who act with us to feel that, unless thy blessing is with us, we cannot succeed, and that, except the Lord build the house, their labor is but lost that build it. Direct us, then, O Lord, in this and all our doings with thy most gracious favor, and further us with thy continual help, that in all our works begun, continued, and ended in thee, we may glorify thy Name; through Jesus Christ. *Amen.* [PPB, NO. 91][21]

The quickening spirit

All through this day, O Lord, let me touch as many lives as possible for thee; and every life I touch, do thou, by thy Holy Spirit, quicken, whether through the word I speak, the prayer I breathe, the letters I write, or the life I live; in the name of Jesus Christ. *Amen.* [PPB, NO. 33][22]

In controversy

O Lord and Savior Christ, Who camest not to strive nor cry, give unto me, in whatsoever contention I may be, a wise, a sober, a patient, an understanding, a peaceable, a courageous heart. Grant me always to speak thy truth in love, and so to present it that it may be loved; for thy mercies' sake. *Amen.* [PPB, NO. 36][23]

For one lonely after a divorce

O God, who art merciful with our weakness and patient with our pride, help this thy servant, we beseech thee, in the brokenness of *his* home and in the loneliness of *his* heart. Give *him* penitence for *his* wrong choices, thankfulness for thy goodness in the past, and a will to serve thee gladly in the years that lie ahead; through Jesus Christ our Lord. *Amen.* [PPB, NO. 117][14]

For courage

Fortify us, O God, with the courage which cometh only from thee; that in the midst of all our perils and perplexities we may find that peace which only thou canst give; through Jesus Christ our Lord. *Amen.*   [PPB, NO. 278][13]

For parents of a retarded child

O God of mercy and compassion, behold and bless these people in their need; fold their child in the arms of thy love; take away all bitterness from their hearts and give them patience, kindness, and wisdom to choose wisely for their child who is a whole person in thy sight; in the name of Jesus Christ our Savior. *Amen.*   [PPB, NO. 248][14]

For inward calm

Serene Son of God, whose will subdued the troubled waters and laid to rest the fears of men: Let thy majesty master us, thy power of calm control us; that for our fears we may have faith, and for our disquietude perfect trust in thee; who dost live and govern all things, world without end. *Amen.*   [PPB, NO. 191][13]

For consecration of our lives

O God, who alone canst uphold the minds of men, without whose beauty and goodness our souls are unfed, without whose truthfulness our reasons wither; Consecrate our lives to thy will, giving us such purity of heart, such depth of faith, such steadfastness of purpose, that, in thy good time, we may come to think thine own thoughts after thee; through Jesus Christ our Savior. *Amen.*   [PPB, NO. 554][24]

For control of our speech

Almighty God, who knowest how often we sin against thee with our lips; Consecrate our speech to thy service, and keep us often silent, that our hearts may speak to thee and listen for thy voice; through Jesus Christ our Lord. *Amen.* [PPB, NO. 632][20]

In failure

O God, whose blessed Son was despised and rejected of men, help us to accept our failures as real and necessary instructions in our pilgrimage toward freedom and wholeness in Jesus Christ our Savior. *Amen.* [PPB, NO. 572][14]

The tyranny of words

My good Lord Jesus, deliver me from the tyranny of words, that I may hear thee in silence and serve thee with simplicity. *Amen.* [PPB, NO. 562][14]

For restraint in criticism

O Lord, Jesus Christ, who didst show unfailing patience and generosity in thy judgment of the people round thee; Forgive us the careless criticism and unkind words which cause so much suffering to others; help us neither to coin cruel gossip nor give currency to it, but rather to seek the best that lies in everyone and use it to the glory of thy Name. *Amen.* [PPB, NO. 633][25]

For youth

O God, who hast made us in thy image, we give thee thanks for friends and homes, for youth and strength, for hopes and dreams; help us to be honest, to live up to the best we know, and to grow in the knowledge and love of thy Son our Savior Jesus Christ. *Amen.*   [PPB, NO. 62][14]

For all who are without faith

Almighty God, look upon those who have not come to know thee or who do not acknowledge thee: on those who are confused in mind and doubt thee because of life's bewilderments and riddles, or who do not think of thee or turn to thee because of its entanglements and pressures: and on those who even while professing faith yet live without it.

Speak to them, O God, by whatever voices they can hear and heed; let them be enlightened by the witness of all who herald and exemplify thy truth; let them be upheld by the prayers of all who pray believing; and bring them to the haven where unknowing they would be; through Jesus Christ our Lord. *Amen.*   [PPB, NO. 437][26]

For the desolate and lonely

Have compassion, O most merciful Lord, on all who are lonely and desolate. Be thou their Comforter and Friend; give them such earthly solace as thou seest to be best for them; and bring them to the fuller knowledge of thy love; for the sake of Jesus Christ our Lord. *Amen.*   [PPB, NO. 170][27]

For God's love in our life

O God, whose love is our life, open our hearts, we beseech thee, to receive thy gifts; take away from us coldness and calculation, the blindness of pride and the luxury of hurt feelings; pour out upon us thy quickening Spirit, that our dry places may be green again, and our whole being rejoice in thee; through Jesus Christ our Lord. *Amen.*   [PPB, NO. 561][14]

For the despondent

O God, we beseech thee for all who are weighed down with the burdens of this world, for whom there seems little hope; comfort them with the assurance of thy love, give them some token of thy continual care for them and, in thy good time, restore them to a measure of cheerfulness in the good companionship of Jesus Christ our Lord.
Amen.   [PPB, NO. 177][14]

For the nervous and tense

Regard, O Lord, with thy fatherly compassion, all who are disquieted and tense, who cannot lose themselves either in happy work by day or in restful sleep by night, who looking within do not know themselves and looking to thee do not find thee. Lead them, we pray thee, out of clangor into quietude, out of futility into usefulness, out of despair into the sure serenity of truth. Teach them to believe that thou art faithful, and that thy charity hopeth all things and endureth all things; that all the darkness of the world, even the inner blackness of the soul, cannot quench one small candle of fidelity. Give them of thy perspective, thy humor, thy gift of tranquility and poise. Be so patient with them that they may learn to be patient with themselves; so firm, that they may lean on thee; so persistent in leading, that they may venture out and find pasture in the sunny fields of thy kingdom, where all who follow thy shepherding may find gladness and delight; in the name of earth's most calm and daring Son, Word of God, and Master of men, our Savior Jesus Christ.
Amen.   [PPB, NO. 181][13]

For honesty

Almighty God, who lookest upon the inward man, forbid us
in thy presence the vain endeavor to hide from thee what we
have thought and done and truly are. Give us candor to
acknowledge freely to thee what must be forever hidden
from the knowledge of others, and may no false shame keep
us from confessing those sins which no proper shame kept us
from committing; through Jesus Christ our Lord.
Amen.   [PPB, NO. 209][20]

For the needy

Almighty God, look upon those who are in need but cannot
work, or who lack employment and search for it in vain: on
those who struggle to meet exacting claims with inadequate
resources: on all who move in insecurity, attended by worry
or despair. Stand by them, O God, in their deprivations,
their dilemmas, and guide them as they try to solve their
problems; let them come to open doors of opportunity or
refuge; and so quicken and extend the world's concern for all
its people that every man may be ensured a livelihood and
safety from the bitterness of want; through Jesus Christ our
Lord. *Amen.*   [PPB, NO. 183][26]

III
The Family
and Home

The Family and Home

For families and homes

O God our Father, bind together in your all-embracing love
every family on earth. Banish anger and bitterness within
them; nourish forgiveness and peace. Bestow upon parents
such wisdom and patience that they may gently exercise the
disciplines of love, and call forth from their children their
greatest virtue and their highest skill. Instill in children such
independence and self-respect that they may freely obey their
parents, and grow in the joys of companionship. Open ears
to hear the truth within the words another speaks; open eyes
to see the reality beneath another's appearance; and make the
mutual affection of families a sign of your kingdom; through
Jesus Christ our Lord. *Amen.*   [PTL, 56]¹

Almighty Father, from whom every family in heaven and
earth is named: we entreat thy mercy for the families of this
and every land, for man and wife and child, and for all who
have the care of children; that by thy hallowing our homes
may be blessed and our children may grow up in the
knowledge of thee and of thy Son, Jesus Christ our Lord.
Amen.   [PPB, NO. 119]²⁸

Almighty God, our heavenly Father, who settest the solitary
in families: We commend to thy continual care the homes in
which thy people dwell. Put far from them, we beseech thee,

every root of bitterness, the desire of vainglory, and the pride of life. Fill them with faith, virtue, knowledge, temperance, patience, godliness. Knit together in constant affection those who, in holy wedlock, have been made one flesh. Turn the hearts of the parents to the children, and the hearts of the children to the parents; and so enkindle fervent charity among us all, that we may evermore be kindly affectioned one to another; through Jesus Christ our Lord. *Amen.*   [828]

For families in conflict

O God, the true Father of us all, look with compassion on all families living in tension, fear, or strife. Relieve their suspicions, calm their anger, and allay their anxiety. Help them to find the source of their conflicts, and to seek help from you and from those through whom you work; that the bonds of love and patience may be strengthened and rebuilt, and that they may live together in such a way that your Name may be honored and glorified among those around them; through Jesus Christ our Lord. *Amen.*   [PTL, 57][29]

For our family and household

O Eternal God, who alone makest men to be of one mind in a house; Help us faithfully to fulfill our duties as members of our several households. Put far from us all unkind thoughts, anger, and evil speaking. Give us tender hearts, full of affection and sympathy toward all. Grant us grace to feel the sorrows and trials of others as our own, and to bear patiently with their imperfections. Preserve us from selfishness, and grant that, day by day, walking in love, we may grow up into the likeness of thy blessed Son, and be found ready to meet him, and to enter with him into that place which he has gone to prepare for us; for his sake, who liveth and reigneth with thee and the Holy Ghost ever, one God, world without end. *Amen.*   [PPB, NO. 541][20]

94

O Heavenly Father, of whom the whole family in heaven and earth is named; Be present in this house, that all who live here, being kindly affectioned one to another, may find it a haven of blessing and of peace; through Jesus Christ our Lord. *Amen.*   [PPB, NO. 155][30]

Visit, we beseech thee, O Lord this habitation, and drive far from it all snares of the enemy; let thy holy angels dwell herein to preserve us in peace, and let thy blessing be ever upon us; through Jesus Christ our Lord.
Amen.   [PPB, NO. 157][31]

Lord, behold our family here assembled. We thank thee for this place in which we dwell; for the love that unites us; for the peace accorded us this day; for the hope with which we expect the morrow; for the health, the work, the food and the bright skies that make our lives delightful; for our friends in all parts of the earth.

Give us courage, gaiety and the quiet mind. Spare to us our friends, soften to us our enemies. Bless us, if it may be, in all our innocent endeavors. If it may not, give us the strength to encounter that which is to come, that we may be brave in peril, constant in tribulation, temperate in wrath, and in all changes of fortune and down to the gates of death, loyal and loving one to another. *Amen.*   [PPB, NO. 549][32]

Almighty and everlasting God, grant to this home the grace of your presence, that you may be known to be the inhabitant of this dwelling, and the defender of this household; through Jesus Christ our Lord, who with you and the Holy Spirit lives and reigns, one God, for ever and ever. *Amen.*   [BOOS, 131]

Let the mighty power of the Holy God be present in this place to banish from it every unclean spirit, to cleanse it from every residue of evil, and to make it a secure habitation for *those* who *dwell* in it; in the Name of Jesus Christ our Lord. *Amen.*   [BOOS, 132]

Almighty God, who art the author of all goodness, look down in mercy upon this family and household and bless all who belong to it, present or absent. Save and defend us in all dangers and adversities, give us all things that are needful to our souls and bodies, and bring us safely to thy heavenly kingdom; through Jesus Christ our Lord. *Amen.*   [PPB, NO. 543][33]

O eternal God, who settest the solitary in families and fillest the hungry with good things, visit this home and family with thy grace and favor; knit them together in thy love through good times and bad, bless their comings in and their goings out, give them thankful hearts for their daily bread and for each other, and bring them at the last into thy heavenly dwelling place; through Jesus Christ our Lord. *Amen.*   [PPB, NO. 154][14]

Shed the bright rays of thy light, O Father, upon this family and household, that every member of the same, made confident by thy guidance, may fulfill his daily duty with pure motives and a gallant heart. Be close to us in times of stress and strain, that our courage and our hope may never fail. Let thy sheltering arm protect us, that we may be valiant in all peril. Turn for us sorrow into joy, darkness into sunshine, death into life; so that when the evening comes and our work on earth is done, we may pass triumphantly into the uplands of fellowship in thy family above; through Jesus Christ our Lord. *Amen.*   [PPB, NO. 156][34]

Be present with us, O Lord, in our daily duties, and grant to those who dwell in this house the strength and protection of thy continual help; that thou mayest be known as the master of the family and the defender of this home; through Jesus Christ our Lord. *Amen.*   [PPB, NO. 540][35]

Blessing of a home

Our heavenly Father, fill this home with the gladness of thy presence. Bless all who live here with thy gift of love; help them to show forth thy love to each other and to all men. Keep them safe from all evil and bring them to thy heavenly Kingdom. *Amen.*   [PPB, NO. 158][36]

Household prayer at the front door

Sovereign Lord, you are Alpha and Omega, the beginning and the end: Send your *servants* out from this place on many errands, be *their* constant companion in the way, and welcome *them* upon *their* return, so that coming and going *they* may be sustained by your presence, O Christ our Lord. *Amen.*   [BOOS, 133]

Household prayer in a living room or family room

Give your blessing, Lord, to all who share this room, that they may be knit together in fellowship here on earth, and joined with the communion of your saints in heaven; through Jesus Christ our Lord. *Amen.*   [BOOS, 139]

Household prayer in a dining room

Blessed are you, O Lord, King of the universe, for you give us food and drink to sustain our lives: Make us grateful for all your mercies, and mindful of the needs of others; through Jesus Christ our Lord. *Amen.*   [BOOS, 138]

Household prayer in the kitchen

O Lord our God, you supply every need of ours according to your great riches: Bless the hands that work in this place, and give us grateful hearts for daily bread; through Jesus Christ our Lord. *Amen.*   [boos, 137]

Household prayer in a study or library

O God of truth, eternal ground of all that is, beyond space and time yet within them, transcending all things yet pervading them: Show yourself to us, for we go about in ignorance; reveal yourself to us, for it is you that we seek, O Triune God, Father, Son, and Holy Spirit. *Amen.*   [boos, 134]

Household prayer in a bedroom

O God of life and love, the true rest of your people: Sanctify to your *servants their* hours of rest and refreshment, *their* sleeping and *their* waking; and grant that, strengthened by the indwelling of the Holy Spirit, *they* may rise to serve you all the days of *their* life; through Jesus Christ our Lord. *Amen.*   [boos, 135]

Household prayer in a child's room

Heavenly Father, your Son our Savior took young children into his arms and blessed them: Embrace the *child* whose room this is with your unfailing love, protect *him* from all danger, and bring *him* in safety to each new day, until *he greets* with joy the great day of your kingdom; through Jesus Christ our Lord. *Amen.*   [boos, 135]

Household prayer in a guest room

Loving God, you have taught us to welcome one another as Christ welcomed us: Bless those who from time to time share the hospitality of this home. May your fatherly care shield them, the love of your dear Son preserve them from all evil, and the guidance of your Holy Spirit keep them in the way that leads to eternal life; through Jesus Christ our Lord. *Amen.*   [BOOS, 136]

Household prayer in a bathroom

O holy God, in the incarnation of your Son our Lord you made our flesh the instrument of your self-revelation: Give us a proper respect and reverence for our mortal bodies, keeping them clean and fair, whole and sound; that, glorifying you in them, we may confidently await our being clothed upon with spiritual bodies, when that which is mortal is transformed by life; through Jesus Christ our Lord. *Amen.*   [BOOS, 136]

Household prayer in a workroom or workshop

O God, your blessed Son worked with his hands in the carpenter shop in Nazareth: Be present, we pray, with *those* who *work* in this place, that, laboring as *workers* together with you, *they* may share the joy of your creation; through Jesus Christ our Lord. *Amen.*   [BOOS, 137]

Household prayer in a patio or garden

Jesus, our good Companion, on many occasions you withdrew with your friends for quiet and refreshment: Be present with your *servants* in this place, to which *they come* for fellowship and recreation; and make of it, we pray, a place of serenity and peace; in your Name we ask it. *Amen.*   [BOOS, 138]

Household prayer in an oratory or chapel

Almighty God, from you comes every good prayer, and you pour out on those who desire it the spirit of grace and supplication: Deliver your *servants* when *they draw* near to you in this place from coldness of heart and wanderings of mind, that with steadfast thoughts and kindled affections *they* may worship you in spirit and in truth; through Jesus Christ our Lord. *Amen.*   [BOOS, 134]

On one leaving the home

O God, who art in every place beholding the evil and the good, take into thine own keeping our dear one now going into the world of strangers. Give *him* courage, prudence, self-control. Grant *him* a right judgment in all things. Raise up for *him* friends, if it be thy will, and deliver *him* from the snares and sorrows of loneliness by the power and joy of thy Presence. Grant that in every place *he* may find the House of God and the gate of heaven. Safeguard *him* with the ministry of thy never-failing providence, now and always; for the sake of Jesus Christ our Lord. *Amen.*   [PPB, NO. 108][37]

On returning home

Lord of our going out and our coming in, I thank thee for my return home after the day's round. Whatever the day may have asked or given, thou knowest how much I have left undone that I should have done, and how much I have done amiss. Accept it all, I pray thee, as my evening sacrifice. Forgive the faults and failures and, beyond any power of mine, continue and extend whatever has had any promise for thy cause and thy kingdom. Save me from vain regrets and from too much anxiety for the morrow. Bless the quiet hours with those I love, and as I commit them and myself to thee may we all find renewal of spirit in rest and trustful sleep. In Jesus' name. *Amen.*   [PPB, NO. 550][38]

For Christian homes

Visit, be beseech thee, O Lord, our homes, and drive far from them all snares of the enemy: let thy holy Angels dwell therein to preserve us in peace, and let thy blessing be ever upon us; through Jesus Christ our Lord. *Amen.*   [MFP, 271]

For the good use of leisure

O God, in the course of this busy life, give us times of refreshment and peace; and grant that we may so use our leisure to rebuild our bodies and renew our minds, that our spirits may be opened to the goodness of your creation; through Jesus Christ our Lord. *Amen.*   [825]

For old and young

O God, who dost turn the hearts of the fathers unto the children, and hast granted unto youth to see visions and to age to dream dreams: we beseech thee to draw together the old and the young, that in fellowship with thee they may understand and help one another, and in thy service find their perfect freedom; through Jesus Christ our Lord. *Amen.*   [PPB, NO. 225][20]

For parents

Almighty God, heavenly Father, who hast blessed us with the joy and care of children; Give us light and strength so to train them, that they may love whatsoever things are true and lovely and of good report, following the example of their Savior, Jesus Christ. *Amen.*   [PPB, NO. 118][39]

Deliver us, good Lord, from the excessive demands of business and social life that limit family relationships; from the insensitivity and harshness of judgment that prevent understanding; from domineering ways and selfish imposition of our will; from softness and indulgence mistaken for love. Bless us with wise and understanding hearts that we may demand neither too much nor too little, and grant us such a measure of love that we may nurture our children to that fullness of manhood and womanhood which thou hast purposed for them; through Jesus Christ our Lord. *Amen.* [PPB, NO. 547][40]

For children and parents

Heavenly Father, from whom all fatherhood in heaven and earth is named, bless we beseech thee, all children, and give to their parents, and to all in whose charge they may be, thy Spirit of wisdom and love; so that the home in which they grow up may be to them an image of thy Kingdom, and the care of their parents a likeness of thy love; through Jesus Christ our Lord. *Amen.* [PPB, NO. 120][41]

For the necessities of life

Almighty God, the fountain of all wisdom, you know our necessities before we ask and our ignorance in asking: Have compassion on our weakness, and mercifully give us those things which for our unworthiness we dare not, and for our blindness we cannot ask; through the worthiness of your Son Jesus Christ our Lord, who lives and reigns with you and the Holy Spirit, one God, now and for ever. *Amen.* [231]

For young people

Lord Jesus Christ, you increased in wisdom and stature as you grew to manhood: Be a strong companion and guide to all young persons seeking their true freedom as children of God. Establish them in honor and courage. Direct them in

the paths of love. And grant that as they grow in age, they may grow in faith and in knowledge of that abundant life which you have promised to all your servants.
Amen. [PTL, 58][1]

O Lord Jesus Christ, we pray thee that our young people who are growing in independence, may be ready to be guided by thee. May they trust thee who art the truth, and put themselves in thy hands who art the way and the life. Teach them what to aim for, what to believe and what to do, so that their lives may be built on the everlasting verities.
Amen. [PPB, NO. 548][39]

A general intercession

Remember, gracious God, for good my father, mother, brothers, sisters, husband, (wife), children, god-children. Bless all my relations, benefactors and friends (especially _____). Give thy grace and heavenly benediction to the clergy of my parish. Hear me, good Lord, who commends unto thy tender mercy all that labor under trials and afflictions. Have mercy upon this household; and grant that humility and meekness, peace and charity, chastity and purity, may rule therein. Grant that we may so correct and amend ourselves, that we may love, and fear, and serve thee faithfully all our days. Through our Lord and Savior Jesus Christ. *Amen.* [SAPB, 21]

For one who is pregnant

O Lord and giver of life, receive our prayer for N. and for the child she has conceived, that they may happily come to the time of birth, and serving you in all things may rejoice in your loving providence. We ask this through our Lord Jesus Christ, who lives and reigns with you and the Holy Spirit, one God, now and for ever. *Amen.* [BOOS, 142]

For the responsible use of money

O Lord, your Son has taught us that from those to whom
much is given, much will be required: Guide us to obtain our
money honestly, neither injuring our neighbors nor ravaging
your creation. And help us to use wisely what we have, for
the well-being of our families and all people, and for the
strengthening of your kingdom in justice, beauty, and peace;
through Jesus Christ our Lord. *Amen.*   [PTL, 52][10]

For the care of children

Almighty God, heavenly Father, you have blessed us with the
joy and care of children: Give us calm strength and patient
wisdom as we bring them up, that we may teach them to love
whatever is just and true and good, following the example of
our Savior Jesus Christ. *Amen.*   [829]

For a child not yet baptized

O eternal God, you have promised to be a father to a
thousand generations of those who love and fear you: Bless
this child and preserve *his* life; receive *him* and enable *him* to
receive you, that through the Sacrament of Baptism *he* may
become the child of God; through Jesus Christ our Lord.
Amen.   [444]

Before listening to my child

Help me, O God, to listen to this thy child. Help me to hear
what is said and what is unsaid. Help me to be fair-minded,
honest, just and loving, that the truth may be spoken and
received; through Jesus Christ our Lord.
Amen.   [PPB, NO. 197][14]

At the adoption of a child

May God, the Father of all, bless our child *N.*, and us who have given to *him* our family name, that we may live together in love and affection; through Jesus Christ our Lord. *Amen.* [441]

Our Father, who hast bestowed upon us this great privilege of taking to ourselves as one of our own one of thy little ones, to love and care for, and to bring up in thy faith and fear, grant us, we pray thee, the grace to give to *him* the full measure of our devotion, and to set before *him* always a good example of Christian life. Bless us in our growth together, and may our home be enriched in the simple joys that come of loving and serving one another; through Jesus Christ our Lord. *Amen.* [PPB, NO. 105][12]

For absent loved ones

O God, whose fatherly care reaches to the uttermost parts of the earth: We humbly beseech you graciously to behold and bless those whom we love, now absent from us. Defend them from all dangers of soul and body; and grant that both they and we, drawing nearer to you, may be bound together by your love in the communion of your Holy Spirit, and in the fellowship of your saints; through Jesus Christ our Lord. *Amen.* [830]

O Heavenly Father, who hast bestowed upon us the comfort of friends, look lovingly upon our dear ones from whom we are separated. Protect and keep them from all harm; prosper and bless them in all things good. Give them the strength and consolation of companionship with thee, who art ever near to those who put their trust in thee; and grant in thine own good time that we may renew the fellowship of sight and hand; through Jesus Christ our Lord. *Amen.* [PPB, NO. 223][20]

For those we love

Almighty God, we entrust all who are dear to us to your
never-failing care and love, for this life and the life to come,
knowing that you are doing for them better things than we
can desire or pray for; through Jesus Christ our Lord.
Amen.   [831]

On our wedding anniversary

Heavenly Father, we give thee heartfelt thanks, on this
anniversary of the day when we were made one in holy
matrimony, for thy blessing upon us then and for thy
continual mercies until now. We thank thee that our love has
deepened with the passing days and for all the joys of our
home and family life. Renew thy blessing upon us now, we
beseech thee, as we renew our vows of love and loyalty, and
may thy Holy Spirit strengthen us that we may ever remain
steadfast in our faith and in thy service; through Jesus Christ
our Lord. *Amen.*   [PPB, NO. 542][42]

For a birthday

O God, our times are in your hand: Look with favor, we
pray, on your servant N. as *he* begins another year. Grant
that *he* may grow in wisdom and grace, and strengthen *his*
trust in your goodness all the days of *his* life; through Jesus
Christ our Lord. *Amen.*   [830]

Watch over thy child, O Lord, as *his* days increase; bless and
guide *him* wherever *he* may be. Strengthen *him* when *he*
stands; comfort *him* when discouraged or sorrowful; raise
him up if *he* fall; and in *his* heart may thy peace which
passeth understanding abide all the days of *his* life; through
Jesus Christ our Lord. *Amen.*   [830]

At the beginning of each new day

This is another day, O Lord. I know not what it will bring
forth, but make me ready, Lord, for whatever it may be. If I
am to stand up, help me to stand bravely. If I am to sit still,
help me to sit quietly. If I am to lie low, help me to do it
patiently. And if I am to do nothing, let me do it gallantly.
Make these words more than words, and give me the Spirit
of Jesus. *Amen.* [461]

O God, Thou art my God, who hast made me for thyself.
O Lord, Heavenly Father, to thee I devote my heart, and my
entire life. Grant me thy grace, I implore thee, that this day
I may live as in thy presence, and walk in the path of thy
commandments, following the example of my Savior Christ,
and being made like unto him. Give to me thy Holy Spirit
that, trusting only in him, I may overcome those sins which
beset me.

Vouchsafe, O gracious God, to me and to _____ such
blessings as we need both temporal and spiritual. I ask in the
Name and through the merits of Jesus Christ our Lord.
Amen. [SAPB, 12]

Lord God, almighty and everlasting Father, you have
brought us in safety to this new day: Preserve us with your
mighty power, that we may not fall into sin, nor be overcome
by adversity; and in all we do, direct us to the fulfilling of
your purpose; through Jesus Christ our Lord. *Amen.* [100]

At noonday

Blessed Savior, at this hour you hung upon the cross,
stretching out your loving arms: Grant that all the peoples of
the earth may look to you and be saved; for your mercies'
sake. *Amen.* [138]

Evening prayers

Be our light in the darkness, O Lord, and in your great mercy defend us from all perils and dangers of this night; for the love of your only Son, our Savior Jesus Christ. *Amen.*

Be present, O merciful God, and protect us through the hours of this night, so that we who are wearied by the changes and chances of this life may rest in your eternal changelessness; through Jesus Christ our Lord. *Amen.*

Look down, O Lord, from your heavenly throne, and illumine this night with your celestial brightness; that by night as by day your people may glorify your holy Name; through Jesus Christ our Lord. *Amen.*

Visit this place, O Lord, and drive far from it all snares of the enemy; let your holy angels dwell with us to preserve us in peace; and let your blessing be upon us always; through Jesus Christ our Lord. *Amen.*

Keep watch, dear Lord, with those who work, or watch, or weep this night, and give your angels charge over those who sleep. Tend the sick, Lord Christ; give rest to the weary, bless the dying, soothe the suffering, pity the afflicted, shield the joyous; and all for your love's sake. *Amen.*

The almighty and merciful Lord, Father, Son, and Holy Spirit, bless us and keep us. *Amen.* [133-135]

Abide with us

Abide with us, O Lord, for it is toward evening and the day is far spent; abide with us, and with thy whole Church. Abide with us in the evening of the day, in the evening of life, in the evening of the world. Abide with us in thy grace and mercy, in holy Word and Sacrament, in thy comfort and thy blessing. Abide with us in the night of distress and fear, in the night of doubt and temptation, in the night of bitter death, when these shall overtake us. Abide with us and all thy faithful ones, O Lord, in time and in eternity. *Amen.*   [ppb, no. 217][43]

At bedtime

Almighty Father, you give the sun for a light by day, and the moon and the stars by night: Graciously receive us, this night and always, into your favor and protection, defending us from all harm and governing us with your Holy Spirit, that every shadow of ignorance, every failure of faith or weakness of heart, every evil or wrong desire may be removed far from us; so that we, being justified in our Lord Jesus Christ, may be sanctified by your Spirit, and glorified by your infinite mercies in the day of the glorious appearing of our Lord and Savior Jesus Christ. *Amen.*   [boos, 42]

IV
Thanksgivings

Thanksgivings

For the beginning of a new day

Almighty and everlasting God, in whom we live and move
and have our being; We, thy needy creatures, render thee our
humble praises, for thy preservation of us from the beginning
of our lives to this day, and especially for having delivered us
from the dangers of the past night. For these thy mercies, we
bless and magnify thy glorious Name; humbly beseeching
thee to accept this our morning sacrifice of praise and
thanksgiving; for his sake who lay down in the grave, and
rose again for us, thy Son our Savior Jesus Christ.
Amen. [28BCP, 587]

For our marriage

We thank you, most gracious God, for consecrating our
marriage in Christ's Name and presence. Lead us further in
companionship with each other and with you. Give us grace
to live together in love and fidelity, with care for one another.
Strengthen us all our days, and bring us to that holy table
where, with those we love, we will feast for ever in our
heavenly home; through Jesus Christ our Lord.
Amen. [BOOS, 146]

For the birth of a child

O God, our heavenly Father, we thank you that you have brought your servant *N.* safely through childbirth and have blessed this family with the gift of a son (*or*, a daughter, *or*, children). Grant that by your grace, *his* parents, honoring each other and obeying your will, may make their home an image of your kingdom and cherish *him* in the likeness of your love; through Jesus Christ our Lord. *Amen.*   [PTL, 87][19]

For heroic service

O Judge of the nations, we remember before you with grateful hearts the men and women of our country who in the day of decision ventured much for the liberties we now enjoy. Grant that we may not rest until all the people of this land share the benefits of true freedom and gladly accept its disciplines. This we ask in the Name of Jesus Christ our Lord. *Amen.*   [839]

For the harvest

Most gracious God, by whose knowledge the depths are broken up and the clouds drop down the dew: We yield thee hearty thanks and praise for the return of seedtime and harvest, for the increase of the ground and the gathering in of its fruits, and for all the other blessings of thy merciful providence bestowed upon this nation and people. And, we beseech thee, give us a just sense of these great mercies, such as may appear in our lives by a humble, holy, and obedient walking before thee all our days; through Jesus Christ our Lord, to whom, with thee and the Holy Ghost be all glory and honor, world without end. *Amen.*   [840]

For the mission of the church

Almighty God, you sent your Son Jesus Christ to reconcile the world to yourself: We praise and bless you for those whom you have sent in the power of the Spirit to preach the Gospel to all nations. We thank you that in all parts of the earth a community of love has been gathered together by their prayers and labors, and that in every place your servants call upon your Name; for the kingdom and the power and the glory are yours for ever. *Amen.* [838]

For the gift of a child

Heavenly Father, you sent your own Son into this world. We thank you for the life of this child, *N.*, entrusted to our care. Help us to remember that we are all your children, and so to love and nurture *him*, that *he* may attain to that full stature intended for *him* in your eternal kingdom; for the sake of your dear Son, Jesus Christ our Lord. *Amen.* [841]

For new parents

O God, you have taught us through your blessed Son that whoever receives a little child in the name of Christ receives Christ himself: We give you thanks for the blessing you have bestowed upon this family in giving them a child. Confirm their joy by a lively sense of your presence with them, and give them calm strength and patient wisdom as they seek to bring this child to love all that is true and noble, just and pure, lovable and gracious, excellent and admirable, following the example of our Lord and Savior, Jesus Christ. *Amen.* [443]

For a new mother

O gracious God, we give you humble and hearty thanks
that you have preserved through the pain and anxiety of
childbirth your servant N., who desires now to offer you her
praises and thanksgivings. Grant, most merciful Father, that
by your help she may live faithfully according to your will in
this life, and finally partake of everlasting glory in the life to
come; through Jesus Christ our Lord. *Amen.*   [444]

By the newly baptized

All praise and thanks to you, most merciful Father, for
adopting us as your own children, for incorporating us into
your holy Church, and for making us worthy to share in the
inheritance of the saints in light; through Jesus Christ your
Son our Lord, who lives and reigns with you and the Holy
Spirit, one God, for ever and ever. *Amen.*   [311]

For the newly baptized

Heavenly Father, we thank you that by water and the Holy
Spirit you have bestowed upon *these* your *servants* the
forgiveness of sin, and have raised *them* to the new life of
grace. Sustain *them*, O Lord, in your Holy Spirit. Give *them*
an inquiring and discerning heart, the courage to will and to
persevere, a spirit to know and to love you, and the gift of joy
and wonder in all your works. *Amen.*   [308]

For the newly confirmed

Almighty God, we thank you that by the death and
resurrection of your Son Jesus Christ you have overcome sin
and brought us to yourself, and that by the sealing of your
Holy Spirit you have bound us to your service. Renew in
these your *servants* the covenant you made with *them* at

their Baptism. Send *them* forth in the power of that Spirit to perform the service you set before *them*; through Jesus Christ your Son our Lord, who lives and reigns with you and the Holy Spirit, one God, now and for ever. *Amen.*   [309]

After Communion at a Eucharist in the home

How wonderful you are, O gracious God, in all your dealings with your people! We praise you now, and give you thanks, because in the blessed Sacrament of the Body and Blood of our Savior Jesus Christ you have visited this house and hallowed it by your presence. Stay among us, we pray, to bind us together in your love and peace. May we serve you, and others in your name; through Jesus Christ our Lord. *Amen.*   [BOOS, 141]

After Communion at an Ordination

Almighty Father, we thank you for feeding us with the holy food of the Body and Blood of your Son, and for uniting us through him in the fellowship of your Holy Spirit. We thank you for raising up among us faithful servants for the ministry of your Word and Sacraments. We pray that N. may be to us an effective example in word and action, in love and patience, and in holiness of life. Grant that we, with *him*, may serve you now, and always rejoice in your glory; through Jesus Christ your Son our Lord, who lives and reigns with you and the Holy Spirit, one God, now and for ever. *Amen.*   [523]

After Communion at a Burial

Almighty God, we thank you that in your great love you have fed us with the spiritual food and drink of the Body and Blood of your Son Jesus Christ, and have given us a foretaste of your heavenly banquet. Grant that this Sacrament may be to us a comfort in affliction, and a pledge of our inheritance in that kingdom where there is no death, neither sorrow nor crying, but the fullness of joy with all your saints; through Jesus Christ our Savior. *Amen.*   [498]

After Communion at a Marriage

O God, the giver of all that is true and lovely and gracious: We give you thanks for binding us together in these holy mysteries of the Body and Blood of your Son Jesus Christ. Grant that by your Holy Spirit, N. and N., now joined in Holy Matrimony, may become one in heart and soul, live in fidelity and peace, and obtain those eternal joys prepared for all who love you; for the sake of Jesus Christ our Lord. *Amen.*   [432]

For deliverance from sin

We thank you, heavenly Father, that you have delivered us from the dominion of sin and death and brought us into the kingdom of your Son; and we pray that, as by his death he has recalled us to life, so by his love he may raise us to eternal joys; who lives and reigns with you, in the unity of the Holy Spirit, one God, now and for ever. *Amen.*   [224]

For the diversity of races and cultures

O God, who created all peoples in your image, we thank you for the wonderful diversity of races and cultures in this world. Enrich our lives by ever-widening circles of fellowship, and show us your presence in those who differ most from us, until our knowledge of your love is made perfect in our love for all your children; through Jesus Christ our Lord. *Amen.*   [840]

For the faithful departed

Almighty God, with whom still live the spirits of those who
die in the Lord, and with whom the souls of the faithful are
in joy and felicity: We give you heartfelt thanks for the good
examples of all your servants, who, having finished their
course in faith, now find rest and refreshment. May we, with
all who have died in the true faith of your holy Name, have
perfect fulfillment and bliss in your eternal and everlasting
glory, through Jesus Christ our Lord. *Amen.*   [503]

For the saints and faithful departed

We give thanks to you, O Lord our God, for all your servants
and witnesses of time past: for Abraham, the father of
believers, and Sarah his wife; for Moses, the lawgiver, and
Aaron, the priest; for Miriam and Joshua, Deborah and
Gideon, and Samuel with Hannah his mother; for Isaiah and
all the prophets; for Mary, the mother of our Lord; for Peter
and Paul and all the apostles; for Mary and Martha, and
Mary Magdalene; for Stephen, the first martyr, and all the
martyrs and saints in every age and in every land. In your
mercy, O Lord our God, give us, as you gave to them, the
hope of salvation and the promise of eternal life; through
Jesus Christ our Lord, the first-born of many from the dead.
Amen.   [838]

For peacemakers

Lord Jesus Christ, O Prince of Peace, you have revealed to us
the vision of one world where all live together as children of
one Father: We thank you for those who, following in your
footsteps, have drawn our hearts to an understanding of
common needs, and have challenged us to live generously.
Confirm in us our purpose to obey your will, that our world
may become the kingdom of your righteousness, now and for
ever. *Amen.*   [PTL, 85][19]

After Communion

Almighty and everliving God,
we thank you for feeding us with the spiritual food
of the most precious Body and Blood
of your Son our Savior Jesus Christ;
and for assuring us in these holy mysteries
that we are living members of the Body of your Son,
and heirs of your eternal kingdom.
And now, Father, send us out
to do the work you have given us to do,
to love and serve you
as faithful witnesses of Christ our Lord.
To him, to you, and to the Holy Spirit,
be honor and glory, now and for ever.
Amen. [366]

Gracious Father, we give you praise and thanks for this Holy
Communion of the Body and Blood of your beloved Son
Jesus Christ, the pledge of our redemption; and we pray that
it may bring us forgiveness of our sins, strength in our
weakness, and everlasting salvation; through Jesus Christ
our Lord. *Amen.* [399]

Almighty and everliving God, we most heartily thank thee
for that thou dost feed us, in these holy mysteries, with the
spiritual food of the most precious Body and Blood of thy
Son our Savior Jesus Christ; and dost assure us thereby of
thy favor and goodness towards us; and that we are very
members incorporate in the mystical body of thy Son, the
blessed company of all faithful people; and are also heirs,
through hope, of thy everlasting kingdom. And we humbly
beseech thee, O heavenly Father, so to assist us with thy
grace, that we may continue in that holy fellowship, and do
all such good works as thou hast prepared for us to walk in;
through Jesus Christ our Lord, to whom, with thee and the
Holy Ghost, be all honor and glory, world without end.
Amen. [339]

Eternal God, heavenly Father,
you have graciously accepted us as living members
of your Son our Savior Jesus Christ,
and you have fed us with spiritual food
in the Sacrament of his Body and Blood.
Send us now into the world in peace,
and grant us strength and courage
to love and serve you
with gladness and singleness of heart;
through Christ our Lord.
Amen. [365]

For the beauty of the earth

We give you thanks, most gracious God, for the beauty of
earth and sky and sea; for the richness of mountains, plains,
and rivers; for the songs of birds and the loveliness of
flowers. We praise you for these good gifts, and pray that we
may safeguard them for our posterity. Grant that we may
continue to grow in our grateful enjoyment of your abundant
creation, to the honor and glory of your Name, now and for
ever. *Amen.* [840]

For a beginning of recovery from illness

O Lord, your compassions never fail and your mercies are
new every morning: We give you thanks for giving our
brother (sister) N. both relief from pain and hope of health
renewed. Continue in *him*, we pray, the good work you have
begun; that *he*, daily increasing in bodily strength, and
rejoicing in your goodness, may so order *his* life and conduct
that *he* may always think and do those things that please
you; through Jesus Christ our Lord. *Amen.* [460]

For the widening vision of social justice

O God of righteousness, we thank you for the faith we inherit. It gives us the vision of a world where children of God are not ground down in oppression but lifted up in freedom. We thank you for the gift of your love. It demands that the human person must not be bound in misery but liberated in joy. We thank you for the abundance of the earth. It makes possible a society of persons not equal in poverty but diverse in wealth. We thank you for the pricking of conscience. It makes us lay the foundations for such a world, not tomorrow but today. We thank you in the Name of Jesus Christ our Lord. *Amen.*   [PTL, 85][19]

For the restoration of peace

Almighty God, whose Name is Love: With full hearts we thank you for peace restored, and for the light which shines through the darkness of the world's sin. We thank you for preserving our lives in the perils and dangers through which we have passed, and for opening before us a new opportunity to establish justice among our brothers. Give us grace to love all men as your Son loved us, and so make us worthy to live in peace, both now and for ever. *Amen.*   [PTL, 84][9]

For the restoration of domestic peace

O God of justice and peace, we thank you for the settlement of strife recently accomplished among us. Grant that the terms of agreement may be implemented in good faith, to our mutual benefit and to the honor of your holy Name; through Jesus Christ our Lord. *Amen.*   [PTL, 84][19]

O Eternal God, our heavenly Father, who alone makest men to be of one mind in a house, and stillest the outrage of a violent and unruly people; We bless thy holy Name, that it hath pleased thee to appease the seditious tumults which have been lately raised up amongst us; most humbly beseeching thee to grant to all of us grace, that we may henceforth obediently walk in thy holy commandments; and, leading a quiet and peaceable life in all godliness and honesty, may continually offer unto thee our sacrifice of praise and thanksgiving for these thy mercies towards us; through Jesus Christ our Lord. *Amen.*   [28BCP, 52]

For rain

O God, our heavenly Father, by whose gracious providence the former and the latter rain descend upon the earth, that it may bring forth fruit for the use of man; We give thee humble thanks that it hath pleased thee to send us rain to our great comfort, and to the glory of thy holy Name; through Jesus Christ our Lord. *Amen.*   [28BCP, 51]

For a safe return from travel

Heavenly Father, we thank you for this journey (*or,* these journeys) safely ended, and for the many persons who have served us in our travel. We thank you for your guiding hand, preserving us from dangers, seen and unseen, along the way, and for your presence at every destination. Grant that our wisdom in ordering our lives may increase as fast as our skill in conquering distance, so that all our journeys may be undertaken with care and ended with praise; through Jesus Christ our Lord. *Amen.*   [PTL, 88][19]

Most gracious Lord, whose mercy is over all thy works; We praise thy holy Name that thou hast been pleased to conduct in safety, through the perils of the great deep (of *his* way), *this* thy *servant,* who now *desireth* to return *his* thanks unto thee in thy holy Church. May *he* be duly sensible of thy merciful providence towards *him*, and ever express *his* thankfulness by a holy trust in thee, and obedience to thy laws; through Jesus Christ our Lord. *Amen.*   [28BCP, 53]

General thanksgivings

Accept, O Lord, our thanks and praise for all that you have done for us. We thank you for the splendor of the whole creation, for the beauty of this world, for the wonder of life, and for the mystery of love.

We thank you for the blessing of family and friends, and for the loving care which surrounds us on every side.

We thank you for setting us at tasks which demand our best efforts, and for leading us to accomplishments which satisfy and delight us.

We thank you also for those disappointments and failures that lead us to acknowledge our dependence on you alone.

Above all, we thank you for your Son Jesus Christ; for the truth of his Word and the example of his life; for his steadfast obedience, by which he overcame temptation; for his dying, through which he overcame death; and for his rising to life again, in which we are raised to the life of your kingdom.

Grant us the gift of your Spirit, that we may know him and make him known; and through him, at all times and in all places, may give thanks to you in all things. *Amen.*   [836]

Almighty God, Father of all mercies,
we your unworthy servants give you humble thanks
for all your goodness and loving-kindness
to us and to all whom you have made.
We bless you for our creation, preservation,
and all the blessings of this life;
but above all for your immeasurable love
in the redemption of the world by our Lord Jesus Christ;

for the means of grace, and for the hope of glory.
And, we pray, give us such an awareness of your mercies,
that with truly thankful hearts we may show forth your praise,
not only with our lips, but in our lives,
by giving up our selves to your service,
and by walking before you
in holiness and righteousness all our days;
through Jesus Christ our Lord,
to whom, with you and the Holy Spirit,
be honor and glory throughout all ages.
Amen. [101]

To our prayers, O Lord, we join our unfeigned thanks for
all thy mercies; for our being, our reason, and all other
endowments and faculties of soul and body; for our health,
friends, food, and raiment, and all the other comforts and
conveniences of life. Above all, we adore thy mercy in
sending thy only Son into the world, to redeem us from sin
and eternal death, and in giving us the knowledge and sense
of our duty towards thee. We bless thee for thy patience with
us, notwithstanding our many and great provocations; for all
the directions, assistances, and comforts of thy Holy Spirit;
for thy continual care and watchful providence over us
through the whole course of our lives; and particularly for
the mercies and benefits of the past day; beseeching thee to
continue these thy blessings to us, and to give us grace to
show our thankfulness in a sincere obedience to his laws,
through whose merits and intercession we received them all,
thy Son our Savior Jesus Christ. *Amen.* [28BCP, 591]

For the end of dearth and scarcity

O most merciful Father, who of thy gracious goodness hast
heard the devout prayers of thy Church, and turned our
dearth and scarcity into plenty; We give thee humble thanks

for this thy special bounty; beseeching thee to continue thy loving-kindness unto us, that our land may yield us her fruits of increase, to thy glory and our comfort; through Jesus Christ our Lord. *Amen.*   [28BCP, 51]

For deliverance from our enemies

O Almighty God, who art a strong tower of defense unto thy servants against the face of their enemies; We yield thee praise and thanksgiving for our deliverance from those great and apparent dangers wherewith we were compassed. We acknowledge it thy goodness that we were not delivered over as a prey unto them; beseeching thee still to continue such thy mercies towards us, that all the world may know that thou art our Savior and mighty Deliverer; through Jesus Christ our Lord. *Amen.*   [28BCP, 52]

For the restoration of health

Almighty God and heavenly Father, we give you humble thanks because you have been graciously pleased to deliver from *his* sickness *your servant* N., in whose behalf we bless and praise your Name. Grant, O gracious Father, that *he*, through your help, may live in this world according to your will, and also be a partaker of everlasting glory in the life to come; through Jesus Christ our Lord. *Amen.*   [841]

O God, who art the giver of life, of health, and of safety; We bless thy Name, that thou hast been pleased to deliver from *his* bodily sickness *this* thy *servant*, who now *desireth* to return thanks unto thee, in the presence of all thy people. Gracious art thou, O Lord, and full of compassion to the children of men. May *his heart* be duly impressed with a sense of thy merciful goodness, and may *he* devote the residue of *his* days to an humble, holy, and obedient walking before thee; through Jesus Christ our Lord. *Amen.* [28BCP, 52]

For fair weather

O Lord God, who hast justly humbled us by thy late visitation of us with immoderate rain and waters, and in thy mercy hast relieved and comforted our souls by this seasonable and blessed change of weather; We praise and glorify thy holy Name for this thy mercy, and will always declare thy loving-kindness from generation to generation; through Jesus Christ our Lord. *Amen.* [28BCP, 51]

In the evening

O God, the life of all who live, the light of the faithful, the strength of those who labor, and the repose of the dead: We thank you for the blessings of the day that is past, and humbly ask for your protection through the coming night. Bring us in safety to the morning hours; through him who died and rose again for us, your Son our Savior Jesus Christ. *Amen.* [124]

Almighty God, we give you thanks for surrounding us, as daylight fades, with the brightness of the vesper light; and we implore you of your great mercy that, as you enfold us with the radiance of this light, so you would shine into our hearts the brightness of your Holy Spirit; through Jesus Christ our Lord. *Amen.* [110]

Blessed are you, O Lord, the God of our fathers, creator of the changes of day and night, giving rest to the weary, renewing the strength of those who are spent, bestowing upon us occasions of song in the evening. As you have protected us in the day that is past, so be with us in the coming night; keep us from every sin, every evil, and every fear; for you are our light and salvation, and the strength of our life. To you be glory for endless ages. *Amen.* [113]

A thanksgiving

Almighty God, Father of all mercies, we thank thee for all thou hast given and for all thou hast forgiven; for thy hidden blessings and for those which in our negligence we have passed over: for every gift of nature or of grace: for our power of loving: for all which thou hast yet in store for us: for everything, whether joy or sorrow, whereby thou art drawing us to thyself through Jesus Christ our Lord. *Amen.*   [PPB, NO. 451][44]

For God's best gifts

O God of Love, we yield thee thanks for whatsoever thou hast given us richly to enjoy, for health and vigor, for the love and care of home, for joys of friendship, and for every good gift of happiness and strength. We praise thee for all thy servants who by their example and encouragement have helped us on our way, and for every vision of thyself which thou hast ever given us in sacrament or prayer; and we humbly beseech thee that all these thy benefits we may use in thy service and to the glory of thy Holy Name; through Jesus Christ, thy Son, our Lord. *Amen.*   [PPB, NO. 464][15]

Remembering a pastor

Heavenly Father, Shepherd of your people, we thank you for your servant N., who was faithful in the care and nurture of your flock; and we pray that, following his example and the teaching of his holy life, we may by your grace grow into the stature of the fullness of our Lord and Savior Jesus Christ; who lives and reigns with you and the Holy Spirit, one God, for ever and ever. *Amen.*   [248]

Remembering a missionary

Almighty and everlasting God, we thank you for your servant N., whom you called to preach the Gospel to the people of _____ (*or* to the _____ people). Raise up in this and every land evangelists and heralds of your kingdom, that your Church may proclaim the unsearchable riches of our Savior Jesus Christ; who lives and reigns with you and the Holy Spirit, one God, now and for ever. *Amen.*   [247]

For the Church

O God, whose glory fills the skies, I laud and praise thy Holy Name for all the blessings brought to me and to all men in thy holy Church, especially within our own part of it; I bless thee for the gifts of faith, knowledge, and of a whole mind; for the grace of membership and the joy of fellowship; may the operation of thy Sacraments so knit us all to thee in grace that we may be able without fear or hesitation to behold thy wonders in nature. Through Jesus Christ our Lord. *Amen.*   [SAPB, 47]

An act of praise

To God the Father, who first loved us and made us accepted in the Beloved; To God the Son, who loved us and washed us from our sins in his own Blood; To God the Holy Ghost, who sheds the love of God abroad in our hearts — Be all love, and all glory, for time and for eternity. *Amen.*   [SAPB, 47]

For a happy home

O God, our Father, we thank thee for our home and family; for love and forbearance, for friends and foes, for laughter enjoyed and sorrow shared, for the daily bread of thy bounty in good times and bad. Help us to be mindful of thy gifts and glad to show forth thy praise; through Jesus Christ our Lord. *Amen.* [PPB, NO. 545][14]

For our child

We thank thee, O God our Father, for giving us this our child to bring up for thee. Help us as true disciples to set *him* a good example in all we think or say or do. Keep *him* well in body and mind; and grant that *he* may grow in grace and in the knowledge and love of thy Son, our Savior, Jesus Christ. *Amen.* [PPB, NO. 546][15]

V
The Church and Ministry

The Church and Ministry

For the Church

Gracious Father, we pray for thy holy Catholic Church.
Fill it with all truth, in all truth with all peace. Where it is
corrupt, purify it; where it is in error, direct it; where in any
thing it is amiss, reform it. Where it is right, strengthen it;
where it is in want, provide for it; where it is divided, reunite
it; for the sake of Jesus Christ thy Son our Savior.
Amen.   [816]

For Church renewal

Everliving God, whose will it is that all should come to you
through your Son Jesus Christ: Inspire our witness to him,
that all may know the power of his forgiveness and the hope
of his resurrection; who lives and reigns with you and the
Holy Spirit, one God, now and for ever. *Amen.*   [816]

For Church unity

O God the Father of our Lord Jesus Christ, our only Savior,
the Prince of Peace: Give us grace seriously to lay to heart the
great dangers we are in by our unhappy divisions; take away
all hatred and prejudice, and whatever else may hinder us
from godly union and concord; that, as there is but one Body
and one Spirit, one hope of our calling, one Lord, one Faith,

one Baptism, one God and Father of us all, so we may be all of one heart and of one soul, united in one holy bond of truth and peace, of faith and charity, and may with one mind and one mouth glorify THEE; through Jesus Christ our Lord. *Amen.*   [818]

For Church growth

God and Father of all believers, for the glory of your Name multiply, by the grace of the Paschal sacrament, the number of your children; that your Church may rejoice to see fulfilled your promise to our father Abraham; through Jesus Christ our Lord. *Amen.*   [289]

For the Church family

Almighty and everlasting God, by whose Spirit the whole body of your faithful people is governed and sanctified: Receive our supplications and prayers which we offer before you for all members of your holy Church, that in their vocation and ministry they may truly and devoutly serve you; through our Lord and Savior Jesus Christ. *Amen.*   [100]

For the Church in the world

Almighty and everlasting God, in Christ you have revealed your glory among the nations: Preserve the works of your mercy, that your Church throughout the world may persevere with steadfast faith in the confession of your Name; through Jesus Christ our Lord, who lives and reigns with you and the Holy Spirit, one God, for ever and ever. *Amen.*   [235]

For power in mission

Grant, O merciful God, that your Church, being gathered together in unity by your Holy Spirit, may show forth your power among all peoples, to the glory of your Name; through Jesus Christ our Lord, who lives and reigns with you and the Holy Spirit, one God, for ever and ever. *Amen.* [232]

For effective ministry

Keep, O Lord, your household the Church in your steadfast faith and love, that through your grace we may proclaim your truth with boldness, and minister your justice with compassion; for the sake of our Savior Jesus Christ, who lives and reigns with you and the Holy Spirit, one God, now and for ever. *Amen.* [230]

For the mission of the Church

O God, you have made of one blood all the peoples of the earth, and sent your blessed Son to preach peace to those who are far off and to those who are near: Grant that people everywhere may seek after you and find you, bring the nations into your fold, pour out your Spirit upon all flesh, and hasten the coming of your kingdom; through Jesus Christ our Lord, who lives and reigns with you and the Holy Spirit, one God, now and for ever. *Amen.* [257]

Ever-loving God, whose will it is that all men shall come to the knowledge of your Son Jesus Christ, and the power of his forgiveness, and the hope of his resurrection: Grant that in our witness to him we may make worthy use of the means you have given us; and prosper our efforts to share this glad news throughout the world; to the honor of your Name. *Amen.* [PTL, 33][19]

For clergy and people

Almighty and everlasting God, from whom cometh every good and perfect gift: Send down upon our bishops, and other clergy, and upon the congregations committed to their charge, the healthful Spirit of thy grace; and, that they may truly please thee, pour upon them the continual dew of thy blessing. Grant this, O Lord, for the honor of our Advocate and Mediator, Jesus Christ. *Amen.*   [817]

For the presiding bishop, executive council, and staff

Almighty God, giver of wisdom, you never fail to answer the prayers of those who seek you: Bless *N.*, our Presiding Bishop, the Executive Council, and the staff who assist them in their work. Enlighten their minds, grant them patience and insight, and fill them with faith and obedience to your will; that, through your Spirit, they may enable this Church to carry out its mission in the world; through Jesus Christ our Lord. *Amen.*   [PTL, 35][45]

For ecumenism

As Scripture has told us that there is but one God, and one mediator between God and his people, namely Jesus Christ, who has given himself as a ransom for all; Help us, dear Lord, in our attempts at responding to your Oneness by finding a unity in our diversity. We pray in the Name of God who is three in one, Father, Son, and Holy Spirit, before whose Name every knee shall bow as one: Jesus Christ our Lord and Savior. *Amen.*   [DCS]

For denominational leaders

Shepherd my sheep is your command, dear God. In light of that command we ask your help for all denominational leaders who seek to implement the orderly and effective shepherding of your people. Help them in their various tasks that they may be motivated by the words and actions of your Son, Jesus Christ, our Savior. *Amen.* [DCS]

For all clergy

Dear Lord, you have told us, "Beseech the Lord of the harvest to send forth laborers into His harvest." We respond to that request by asking you to equip all clergy with the strength and courage to minister to all your people. Lead them to your Word, send them to your people, and bring us all to your heavenly home. In the Name of Christ Jesus we pray. *Amen.* [DCS]

For church synods and conferences

Almighty Father, we have gathered together in your Name and presence to do the business of your church. Through your Scripture we read that faith without works is dead. Help us in our deliberations that we might stay centered in our faith, but directed from that faith to do your necessary works. Make our concerns your concerns, our desires your desires, our actions your actions, and all to the praise and glory of your Name. *Amen.* [DCS]

For a church convention

Almighty and everlasting Father, you have given the Holy Spirit to abide with us for ever: Bless, we pray, with his grace and presence, the bishops and the other clergy and the laity here (*or* now, *or* soon to be) assembled in your Name, that your Church, being preserved in true faith and godly discipline, may fulfill all the mind of him who loved it and gave himself for it, your Son Jesus Christ our Savior; who lives and reigns with you, in the unity of the Holy Spirit, one God, now and for ever. *Amen.*   [255]

For deputies and delegates to conventions

Eternal Lord God, who by the Holy Spirit presided at the council of the Apostles to guide them in all knowledge and truth: Be present with the Deputies of this diocese soon to be assembled in General Convention. In the passions of debate give them a quiet spirit, in the complexities of the issues give them clear minds, and in the moments of decision give them courageous hearts. Guide them in all things to seek only your glory and the good of your Church; through Jesus Christ our Lord. *Amen.*   [BOOS, 164]

For the diocese

O God, by your grace you have called us in this Diocese to a goodly fellowship of faith. Bless our Bishop(s) N. (and N.), and other clergy, and all our people. Grant that your Word may be truly preached and truly heard, your Sacraments faithfully administered and faithfully received. By your Spirit, fashion our lives according to the example of your Son, and grant that we may show the power of your love to all among whom we live; through Jesus Christ our Lord. *Amen.*   [817]

For our parish family

Almighty and everliving God, ruler of all things in heaven and earth, hear our prayers for this parish family. Strengthen the faithful, arouse the careless, and restore the penitent. Grant us all things necessary for our common life, and bring us all to be of one heart and mind within your holy Church; through Jesus Christ our Lord. *Amen.*   [817]

For election of a bishop or minister

Almighty God, giver of every good gift: Look graciously on your Church, and so guide the minds of those who shall choose a bishop for this Diocese (*or*, rector for this parish), that we may receive a faithful pastor, who will care for your people and equip us for our ministries; through Jesus Christ our Lord. *Amen.* [818]

For a new minister

Everliving God, strengthen and sustain *N.*, that with patience and understanding *he* may love and care for your people; and grant that together they may follow Jesus Christ, offering to you their gifts and talents; through him who lives and reigns with you and the Holy Spirit, one God, for ever and ever. *Amen.* [560]

For choice of fit persons for the ministry

O God, you led your holy apostles to ordain ministers in every place: Grant that your Church, under the guidance of the Holy Spirit, may choose suitable persons for the ministry of Word and Sacrament, and may uphold them in their work for the extension of your kingdom; through him who is the Shepherd and Bishop of our souls, Jesus Christ our Lord, who lives and reigns with you and the Holy Spirit, one God, for ever and ever. *Amen.* [256]

For those to be ordained

Almighty God, the giver of all good gifts, in your divine providence you have appointed various orders in your Church: Give your grace, we humbly pray, to all who are (now) called to any office and ministry for your people; and so fill them with the truth of your doctrine and clothe them with holiness of life, that they may faithfully serve before you, to the glory of your great Name and for the benefit of your holy Church; through Jesus Christ our Lord, who lives and reigns with you, in the unity of the Holy Spirit, one God, now and for ever. *Amen.*   [256]

For a newly consecrated bishop

To you, O Father, all hearts are open; fill, we pray, the heart of *this* your *servant* whom you have chosen to be a bishop in your Church, with such love of you and of all the people, that *he* may feed and tend the flock of Christ, and exercise without reproach the high priesthood to which you have called *him*, serving before you day and night in the ministry of reconciliation, declaring pardon in your Name, offering the holy gifts, and wisely overseeing the life and work of the Church. In all things may *he* present before you the acceptable offering of a pure, and gentle, and holy life; through Jesus Christ your Son, to whom, with you and the Holy Spirit, be honor and power and glory in the Church, now and for ever. *Amen.*   [521]

For a clergy conference

O Lord Jesus Christ, Head of the Church which is thy Body, by whom we have been chosen as ambassadors and ministers of reconciliation, direct us, we beseech thee, in all our doings with thy most gracious favor; let all our plans and purposes be in accordance with thy holy will, our aim only that we may serve thee and our people faithfully as good shepherds of thy flock. Enlighten us by thy Holy Spirit as we consider together the meaning and obligations of our sacred calling, and the opportunities and responsibilities of the Church in these times. Inspire our minds, assist our wills, and strengthen our hands, that we may not falter or fail in the work thou hast given us to do, to thy honor and glory. *Amen.* [PPB, NO. 133][12]

For one whose ministry is ineffective

Almighty God, I thank thee for the vision of service that brought me to thy ministry, and for thy many blessings in the past. Give me patience, I beseech thee, in my dry season; help me to see good will in my people, strengthen my weakness, increase my faith, sustain me in the communion of saints, and restore in me a measure of usefulness in the good companionship of Jesus Christ our Lord. *Amen.* [PPB, NO. 571][14]

For missionaries in other lands

O God our Savior, who willest that all men should be saved and come to the knowledge of the truth: Prosper, we pray thee, our brethren who labor in other lands, (especially those for whom our prayers are desired). Protect them in all perils; support them in loneliness and in the hour of trial; give them grace to bear faithful witness unto thee; and endue them with burning zeal and love, that they may turn many to righteousness, and finally obtain a crown of glory; through Jesus Christ our Lord. *Amen.* [MFP, 266]

For theological seminaries

Almighty God, whose blessed Son called the twelve Apostles and taught them the mysteries of the kingdom of heaven: bless, we beseech thee, those who are preparing for the sacred ministry of thy Church, and those appointed to teach and guide them; that, illuminated with a true understanding

of thy Word and Sacraments, and growing in holiness of life,
they may be made able ministers of the New Covenant, and
may advance thy glory and the salvation of thy elect
servants; through the same Jesus Christ our Lord.
Amen.   [MFP, 265]

For increase of the ministry

O Lord Jesus Christ, whose servants Simon Peter and
Andrew his brother did at thy word straightway leave their
nets to become fishers of men: Give thy grace, we humbly
beseech thee, to those whom thou dost call to the sacred
ministry of thy Church, that they may hear thy voice, and
with glad hearts obey thy word; who livest and reignest with
the Father and the Holy Spirit, one God, world without end.
Amen.   [MFP, 265]

O Almighty God, look mercifully upon the world which thou
hast redeemed by the blood of thy dear Son, and incline the
hearts of many to dedicate themselves to the sacred Ministry
of thy Church; through the same thy Son Jesus Christ our
Lord. *Amen*.   [28BCP, 39]

A pastor's prayer

O Lord my God, I am not worthy to have you come under
my roof; yet you have called your servant to stand in your
house, and to serve at your altar. To you and to your service
I devote myself, body, soul, and spirit. Fill my memory with
the record of your mighty works; enlighten my
understanding with the light of your Holy Spirit; and may all
the desires of my heart and will center in what you would
have me do. Make me an instrument of your salvation for the
people entrusted to my care, and grant that I may faithfully
administer your holy Sacraments, and by my life and

teaching set forth your true and living Word. Be always with me in carrying out the duties of my ministry. In prayer, quicken my devotion; in praises, heighten my love and gratitude; in preaching, give me readiness of thought and expression; and grant that, by the clearness and brightness of your holy Word, all the world may be drawn into your blessed kingdom. All this I ask for the sake of your Son our Savior Jesus Christ. *Amen.* [562]

For a person taking life vows

Blessed are you, O Lord our God, for your great love in sending into the world your only-begotten Son, who for us and for our salvation, emptied himself of his divine estate, and embraced a life apart from the consolations of family, having not even a place to lay his head. We bless your Name, also, that in every age and land you have called men and women to imitate their Lord, by setting zeal for your kingdom and its righteousness ahead of all worldly considerations, the love of your little ones above the claims of flesh and blood, and obedience to your will in place of all personal ambitions.

Accept, we pray, the life profession of this your servant N., who, following the example of the Lord Jesus, of Anna the prophetess and holy Simeon, of the Lady Julian and Nicholas Ferrar (of _____), and of countless others of your saints, now offers *himself* for your service in a life of poverty, chastity, and obedience. Bestow upon *him* your Holy Spirit to dwell in *him* richly, to give *him* steadfastness of purpose, to sanctify *him* more and more fully, and to guide *him* surely into paths of service and of witness, to the honor and glory of your great Name; through Jesus Christ our Lord, who with you and the Holy Spirit lives and reigns, one God, now and for ever. *Amen.* [BOOS, 231]

For religious communities

O Lord Jesus Christ, who saidst: Whoso loseth his life for my sake shall find it: Bestow, we pray thee, thine abundant blessing on those who have left all that they may give themselves to this service, and grant that those whom thou dost call may hear and obey thy voice, and receive the manifold reward which thou hast promised in this time, and in the world to come eternal life. Who livest and reignest, world without end. *Amen.* [SAPB, 39]

For the increase of the religious life

O Lord and lover of souls, pour out, we beseech thee, upon thy Church, as in the old time, the spirit of religious vocation; and grant that those whom thou dost call to give themselves to thee in holy religion may have strength to resist all temptations, and remaining faithful to thee in this life, may obtain thy eternal rewards in the world to come. Through Jesus Christ our Lord. *Amen.* [SAPB, 39]

For a novice

Look with favor, Almighty God, upon this your servant N., who, in response to the prompting of the Holy Spirit, desires to commit *himself* to you in a life of special vocation, and is undertaking to embrace the three-fold path of poverty, chastity, and obedience. Grant *him* the strength of your grace to persevere in *his* endeavor, and the guidance of the Spirit to find *his* true vocation. If it be your will that *he* continue in this way, reveal this to *him*, we pray, and bring *him* in due time to the taking of solemn vows; through Jesus Christ our Lord, who lives and reigns with you and the Holy Spirit, one God, for ever and ever. *Amen.* [BOOS, 230]

Remembering a monastic

O God, whose blessed Son became poor that we through his poverty might be rich: Deliver us from an inordinate love of this world, that we, inspired by the devotion of your servant N., may serve you with singleness of heart, and attain to the riches of the age to come; through Jesus Christ our Lord, who lives and reigns with you, in the unity of the Holy Spirit, one God, now and for ever. *Amen.*   [249]

For monastic orders and vocations

O Lord Jesus Christ, you became poor for our sake, that we might be made rich through your poverty: Guide and sanctify, we pray, those whom you call to follow you under the vows of poverty, chastity, and obedience, that by their prayer and service they may enrich your Church, and by their life and worship may glorify your Name; for you reign with the Father and the Holy Spirit, one God, now and for ever. *Amen.*   [819]

For a retreat

O Lord Jesus Christ, who went apart to pray with your disciples: Grant to your servants in *this* retreat (*or*, in the retreat for _____ in _____) that *we* may rest a while with you and know that you have found us long before. Let the words that shall be spoken here not fall on barren ground, but, enriched by prayer and silence, bear good fruit in our lives to the glory of your holy Name. *Amen.*   [PTL, 38][46]

For a person taking temporary or annual vows

May God the Lord, who called Abraham to leave home and kindred to journey to an unknown destination, and who led the people of Israel by the hand of Moses his servant through the desert to the promised land: Shepherd you in your pilgrimage, and lead you by safe pathways, for his Name's sake. *Amen.*   [BOOS, 230]

May God the Son, who, in his earthly life, was often solitary but never alone, because the Father was with him: Be your constant companion in your withdrawals from the busyness of the world, and support and strengthen you when you return refreshed to bear witness to the love and power of God. *Amen.*   [BOOS, 231]

May God the Holy Spirit, who helps us in our weakness, and intercedes for the saints in accordance with the Father's will: Teach you to pray as you ought to pray; strengthen you in purity of faith, in holiness of life, and in perfectness of love; and bind you ever more and more closely to the Father through the Son. *Amen.*   [BOOS, 231]

And may Almighty God, the holy and undivided Trinity, Father, Son, and Holy Spirit, guard your body, save your soul, and bring you safely to the heavenly country; where he lives and reigns for ever and ever. *Amen.*   [BOOS, 231]

For teachers and catechists

God of all wisdom and knowledge, give your blessing and guidance to all who teach in your Church, that by word and example they may lead those whom they teach to the knowledge and love of you; through Jesus Christ our Lord. *Amen.*   [BOOS, 166]

For church musicians and artists

O God, whom saints and angels delight to worship in heaven: Be ever present with your servants who seek through art and music to perfect the praises offered by your people on earth; and grant to them even now glimpses of your beauty, and make them worthy at length to behold it unveiled for evermore; through Jesus Christ our Lord. *Amen.* [819]

For lay ministers

Have regard to our supplication, O gracious Lord, and confirm with your heavenly benediction your *servants* commissioned to minister in your Church, that with sincere devotion of mind and body *they* may offer acceptable service to you; through Jesus Christ our Lord. *Amen.* [BOOS, 175]

O Lord, without whom our labor is lost: We beseech you to prosper all works in your Church undertaken according to your holy will. Grant to your workers a pure intention, a patient faith, sufficient success on earth, and the blessedness of serving you in heaven; through Jesus Christ our Lord. *Amen.* [BOOS, 176]

For lay readers

Look with favor upon those whom you have called, O Lord, to be Lay Readers in your Church; and grant that they may be so filled with your Holy Spirit that, seeking your glory and the salvation of souls, they may minister your Word with steadfast devotion, and by the constancy of their faith and the innocency of their lives may adorn in all things the doctrine of Christ our Savior; who lives and reigns for ever and ever. *Amen.* [BOOS, 171]

For lectors

Almighty God, whose blessed Son read the Holy Scriptures
in the synagogue: Look graciously upon the lectors of your
Church, and so enlighten them with wisdom and
understanding that they may read your holy Word to the
glory of your Name, and for the building up of your people;
through Jesus Christ our Lord. *Amen.*   [BOOS, 170]

For those who administer the chalice

Grant, Almighty God, that those who minister the cup of
blessing may live in love and holiness according to your
commandment, and at the last come to the joy of your
heavenly feast with all your saints in light; through Jesus
Christ our Lord. *Amen.*   [BOOS, 171]

For choir members

O God, who inspired David the King both to write songs and
to appoint singers for your worship: Give grace to the *singers*
in your Church, that with psalms, and hymns, and spiritual
songs, they may sing and make music to the glory of your
Name; through Jesus Christ our Lord. *Amen.*   [BOOS, 168]

For evangelists

Gracious Father, your Son before he ascended to glory
declared that your people would receive power from the
Holy Spirit to bear witness to him to the ends of the earth:
Be present with all who go forth in his Name. Let your love
shine through their witness, so that the blind may see, the
deaf hear, the lame walk, the dead be raised up, and the poor
have the good news preached to them; through Jesus Christ
our Lord. *Amen.*   [BOOS, 167]

For parish canvassers

Lord Jesus Christ, you sent laborers to prepare for your
coming: Be with all those who go forth in your Name, that
by their witness and commitment the hearts of many will be
turned to you; who live and reign for ever and ever.
Amen. [BOOS, 173]

For parish visitors

O God, your Son Jesus Christ said that we minister to him
when we clothe the naked, give food to the hungry and drink
to the thirsty, and visit the sick and imprisoned: Go with all
those who, following the command of your Christ, visit your
people in his Name; who lives and reigns for ever and ever.
Amen. [BOOS, 172]

For prayer groups

O God, whose Son our Lord on the night of his betrayal
prayed for all his disciples: Hear the prayers of all those who
accept the work and ministry of intercession on behalf of
others, that the needs of many may be met and your will be
done; through Jesus Christ our great High Priest.
Amen. [BOOS, 173]

For officers of church organizations

Regard, O Lord, our supplications, and confirm with your
heavenly benediction your *servants* whom we admit today to
the ministry (office) of _____ ; that with sincere devotion
of mind and body *they* may offer you a service acceptable to
your divine Majesty; through Jesus Christ our Lord.
Amen. [BOOS, 174]

For a women's guild

O God, who hast called us to serve thee with gladness, bless, we beseech thee, the purposes of this group assembled in thy Name; give us charity with one another, generosity in our good works, and devotion to the spread of thy kingdom. *Amen.*   [PPB, NO. 59][14]

For wardens and vestry members

O Eternal God, the foundation of all wisdom and the source of all courage: Enlighten with your grace the Wardens and Vestry of this congregation, and so rule their minds, and guide their counsels, that in all things they may seek your glory and promote the mission of your Church; through Jesus Christ our Lord. *Amen.*   [BOOS, 163]

Almighty God, giver of all gifts, grant to the members of this Vestry, wisdom to avoid false choices, courage to follow our Lord's teachings, vision to see thy true calling for this parish, and the grace humbly to acknowledge thy Church universal, through Jesus Christ our Lord. *Amen.*   [PPB, NO. 56][47]

Blessed Lord, who hath called us to this office in thy Church, guide us, we beseech thee, in our deliberations, so that all our aims and purposes may be to the strengthening of the work in this parish and the support of the Church's mission throughout the world; through Jesus Christ our Lord. *Amen.*   [PPB, NO. 57][12]

For a men's guild

O God, who hast given each of us a man's job to do in thy world, grant that in our being and in our doing we may faithfully and cheerfully accomplish thy will; through Jesus Christ our Lord. *Amen.*   [PPB, NO. 60][14]

For the altar guild

O Loving Savior, we pray thee to send thy blessing upon this Altar Guild and the work of all its members; give us thy grace that we may be loyal to thy Holy Church, and faithful in our care of holy things. Grant that as we adorn and make ready thy Altar we may learn greater love and reverence for all that belongs to thy service, and through all outward symbols come to a clearer vision of the inward and spiritual truth taught by them. We ask this for thy sake, O Blessed Lord and Master. *Amen.*   [PPB, NO. 53][48]

For altar guild members and sacristans

O God, you accepted the service of Levites in your temple, and your Son was pleased to accept the loving service of his friends: Bless the ministry of *these persons* and give *them* grace, that *they*, caring for the vessels and vestments of your worship and the adornment of your sanctuary, may make the place of your presence glorious; through Jesus Christ our Lord. *Amen.*   [BOOS, 166]

For acolytes

O God, our gracious Father: Bless the servers of your Church that they may so serve before your earthly altar in reverence and holiness, that they may attain, with all your saints and angels, the joy of serving you and worshiping you before your Heavenly Altar; through Jesus Christ our Lord. *Amen.*   [BOOS, 165]

For servers and acolytes

Almighty and everlasting God, who givest grace to those who minister; bestow thy blessing, we pray thee, upon thy

servants appointed to serve those who stand before thine
Altar. Give them such seriousness of life, that the services in
which they engage may be to their profit and spiritual good.
Through their association with holy places and things may
they grow in the Christian life, and by their service in the
house where thou dost manifest thine honor and glory,
may they be prepared for that House not made with hands,
eternal in the heavens; through Jesus Christ our Lord.
Amen.   [PPB, NO. 61]⁴⁹

For a young people's group

O God, who hast made us in thy image, we give thee thanks
for friends and homes, for youth and strength, for hopes and
dreams. Help us to be honest, to live up to the best we know,
and to grow in the knowledge and love of thy Son, our Savior
Jesus Christ. *Amen.*   [PPB, NO. 126]¹⁴

For all baptized Christians

Grant, Lord God, to all who have been baptized into the
death and resurrection of your Son Jesus Christ, that, as we
have put away the old life of sin, so we may be renewed in
the spirit of our minds, and live in righteousness and true
holiness; through Jesus Christ our Lord, who lives and reigns
with you, in the unity of the Holy Spirit, one God, now and
for ever. *Amen.*   [252]

Almighty God, by our baptism into the death and
resurrection of your Son Jesus Christ, you turn us from the
old life of sin: Grant that we, being reborn to new life in him,
may live in righteousness and holiness all our days; through
Jesus Christ our Lord, who lives and reigns with you and the
Holy Spirit, one God, now and for ever. *Amen.*   [254]

For catechumens

O God, the creator and savior of all flesh, look with mercy on your *children* whom you call to yourself in love. Cleanse *their hearts* and guard *them* as *they prepare* to receive your Sacraments that, led by your Holy Spirit, *they* may be united with your Son, and enter into the inheritance of your sons and daughters; through Jesus Christ our Lord. *Amen.* [BOOS, 117]

O God of truth, of beauty, and of goodness, we give you thanks that from the beginning of creation you have revealed yourself in the things that you have made; and that in every nation, culture, and language there have been those who, seeing your works, have worshiped you and sought to do your will. Accept our prayers for *these* your *servants* whom you have called to know and love you as you have been perfectly revealed in your Son Jesus Christ our Redeemer, and bring *them* with joy to new birth in the waters of Baptism; through Jesus Christ our Lord. *Amen.* [BOOS, 118]

O God of righteousness and truth, you inaugurated your victory over the forces of deceit and sin by the Advent of your Son: Give to *these catechumens* a growing understanding of the truth as it is in Jesus; and grant that *they*, being cleansed from sin and born again in the waters of Baptism, may glorify with us the greatness of your Name; through Jesus Christ our Lord. *Amen.* [BOOS, 118]

O God, in your pity you looked upon a fallen world, and sent your only Son among us to vanquish the powers of wickedness. Deliver *these* your *servants* from slavery to sin and evil. Purify *their* desires and thoughts with the light of your Holy Spirit. Nourish *them* with your holy Word, strengthen *them* in faith, and confirm *them* in good works; through Jesus Christ our Lord. *Amen.* [BOOS, 118]

Look down in mercy, Lord, upon *these catechumens* now
being taught in your holy Word. Open *their* ears to hear and
their hearts to obey. Bring to *their minds their* past sins,
committed against you and against *their* neighbors, that *they*
may truly repent of them. And in your mercy preserve *them*
in *their* resolve to seek your kingdom and your righteousness;
through Jesus Christ our Lord. *Amen.* [BOOS, 118]

Drive out of *these catechumens*, Lord God, every trace of
wickedness. Protect *them* from the Evil One. Bring *them* to
the saving waters of baptism, and make *them* yours for ever;
through Jesus Christ our Lord. *Amen.* [BOOS, 119]

Lord Jesus Christ, loving Redeemer of all, you alone have the
power to save. At your Name every knee shall bow, whether
in heaven, on earth, or under the earth. We pray to you for
these catechumens who *seek* to serve you, the one true God.
Send your light into *their hearts*, protect *them* from the
hatred of the Evil One, heal in *them* the wounds of sin, and
strengthen *them* against temptation. Give *them* a love of
your commandments, and courage to live always by your
Gospel, and so prepare *them* to receive your Spirit; you who
live and reign for ever and ever. *Amen.* [BOOS, 119]

Most merciful God, behold and sustain *these catechumens*
who *seek* to know you more fully: Free *them* from the grasp
of Satan, and make *them* bold to renounce all sinful desires
that entice *them* from loving you; that, coming in faith to the
Sacrament of Baptism, *they* may commit *themselves* to you,
receive the seal of the Holy Spirit, and share with us in the
eternal priesthood of Jesus Christ our Lord. *Amen.*
[BOOS, 119]

Lord God, unfailing light and source of light, by the death and resurrection of your Christ you have cast out hatred and deceit, and poured upon the human family the light of truth and love: Look upon *these catechumens* whom you have called to enter your covenant, free *them* from the power of the Prince of darkness, and number *them* among the children of promise; through Jesus Christ our Lord. *Amen.* [BOOS, 120]

Stir up, O Lord, the *wills* of *these catechumens*, and assist *them* by your grace, that *they* may bring forth plenteously the fruit of good works, and receive from you a rich reward; through Jesus Christ our Lord. *Amen.* [BOOS, 120]

For candidates for Baptism

Lord God, in the beginning of creation you called forth light to dispel the darkness that lay upon the face of the deep: Deliver *these* your *servants* from the powers of evil and illumine *them* with the light of your presence, that with open eyes and glad hearts *they* may worship you and serve you, now and for ever; through Jesus Christ our Lord. *Amen.* [BOOS, 124]

Lord Christ, true Light who enlightens every one: Shine, we pray, in the *hearts* of *these candidates*, that *they* may clearly see the way that leads to life eternal, and may follow it without stumbling; for you yourself are the Way, O Christ, as you are the Truth and the Life; and you live and reign for ever and ever. *Amen.* [BOOS, 125]

Come, O Holy Spirit, come; come as the wind and cleanse; come as the fire and burn; convict, convert, and consecrate the minds and hearts of *these* your *servants*, to *their* great good and to your great glory; who with the Father and the Son are one God, now and for ever. *Amen.* [BOOS, 125]

O God, you prepared your disciples for the coming of the Spirit through the teaching of your Son Jesus Christ: Make the hearts and minds of your *servants* ready to receive the blessing of the Holy Spirit, that *they* may be filled with the strength of his presence; through Jesus Christ our Lord. *Amen.* [819]

For those about to be baptized

Lord Jesus Christ, you desire that everyone who follows you shall be born again by water and the Spirit: Remember your *servants* (_____) who are soon to be baptized in your Name.

By their names, Lord:
Grant that you will know them, and call them to a life of service. *Amen.*
Grant that they may become the persons you created them to be. *Amen.*
Grant that they may be written for ever in your Book of Life. *Amen.*

Through the water of their baptism, Lord:
Grant that they may be united with you in your death. *Amen.*
Grant that they may receive forgiveness for all their sins. *Amen.*
Grant that they may have power to endure, and strength to have victory in the battle of life. *Amen.*

As members of your Church, Lord:
Grant that they may rise to a new life in the fellowship of those who love you. *Amen.*
Grant that they may suffer when another suffers, and when another rejoices, rejoice. *Amen.*
Grant that they may be your faithful soldiers and servants until their life's end. *Amen.*

Through the abiding presence of your Spirit, Lord:
Grant that they may lead the rest of their lives according to
  this beginning. *Amen.*
Grant that when they pass through the dark waters of death,
  you will be with them. *Amen.*
Grant that they may inherit the kingdom of glory prepared
  for them from the foundation of the world.
  Amen. [PTL, 38][1]

For those about to be confirmed

Almighty God, we thank you that by the death and
resurrection of your Son Jesus Christ you have overcome sin
and brought us to yourself, and that by the sealing of your
Holy Spirit you have bound us to your service. Renew in
these your *servants* the covenant you made with *them* at
their Baptism. Send *them* forth in the power of that Spirit to
perform the service you set before *them*; through Jesus
Christ your Son our Lord, who lives and reigns with you and
the Holy Spirit, one God, now and for ever. *Amen.* [418]

At confirmation

Grant, Almighty God, that we, who have been redeemed
from the old life of sin by our baptism into the death and
resurrection of your Son Jesus Christ, may be renewed in
your Holy Spirit, and live in righteousness and true holiness;
through Jesus Christ our Lord, who lives and reigns with you
and the Holy Spirit, one God, now and for ever.
Amen. [254]

For one reaffirming commitment to Christ

Almighty God, look with favor upon *this person* who *has*
now reaffirmed *his* commitment to follow Christ and to

serve in his name. Give *him* courage, patience, and vision; and strengthen us all in our Christian vocation of witness to the world, and of service to others; through Jesus Christ our Lord. *Amen.* [421]

At a wedding rehearsal

Behold and bless, we beseech thee O God, these people gathered in thy Name and presence: the bride and the groom, those who attend them, their families and their friends. Help us to understand and to accept the blessings of thy love, and give us reverent hearts and minds as we assist in the sacrament of Christian union; through Jesus Christ our Lord. *Amen.* [PPB, NO. 111][14]

For those about to be married

O gracious and everliving God, you have created us male and female in your image: Look mercifully upon this man and this woman who come to you seeking your blessing, and assist them with your grace, that with true fidelity and steadfast love they may honor and keep the promises and vows they make; through Jesus Christ our Savior, who lives and reigns with you in the unity of the Holy Spirit, one God, for ever and ever. *Amen.* [425]

Intercessions at a marriage

Eternal God, creator and preserver of all life, author of salvation, and giver of all grace: Look with favor upon the world you have made, and for which your Son gave his life, and especially upon this man and this woman whom you make one flesh in Holy Matrimony. *Amen.* [429]

Give them wisdom and devotion in the ordering of their common life, that each may be to the other a strength in need, a counselor in perplexity, a comfort in sorrow, and a companion in joy. *Amen.* [429]

Grant that their wills may be so knit together in your will, and their spirits in your Spirit, that they may grow in love and peace with you and one another all the days of their life. *Amen.* [429]

Give them grace, when they hurt each other, to recognize and acknowledge their fault, and to seek each other's forgiveness and yours. *Amen.* [429]

Make their life together a sign of Christ's love to this sinful and broken world, that unity may overcome estrangement, forgiveness heal guilt, and joy conquer despair. *Amen.* [429]

Bestow on them, if it is your will, the gift and heritage of children, and the grace to bring them up to know you, to love you, and to serve you. *Amen.* [429]

Give them such fulfillment of their mutual affection that they may reach out in love and concern for others. *Amen.* [429]

Grant that all married persons who have witnessed these vows may find their lives strengthened and their loyalties confirmed. *Amen.* [430]

Grant that the bonds of our common humanity, by which all your children are united one to another, and the living to the dead, may be so transformed by your grace, that your will may be done on earth as it is in heaven; where, O Father, with your Son and the Holy Spirit, you live and reign in perfect unity, now and for ever. *Amen.* [430]

For the newly married

Almighty God, giver of life and love, bless *N.* and *N.* Grant
them wisdom and devotion in the ordering of their common
life, that each may be to the other a strength in need, a
counselor in perplexity, a comfort in sorrow, and a
companion in joy. And so knit their wills together in your
will and their spirits in your Spirit, that they may live
together in love and peace all the days of their life; through
Jesus Christ our Lord. *Amen.*   [444]

For those renewing marriage vows

O gracious and everliving God, look mercifully on *N.* and
N., who come to renew the promises they have made to each
other. Grant them your blessing, and assist them with your
grace, that with true fidelity and steadfast love they may
honor and keep their promises and vows; through Jesus
Christ our Savior, who lives and reigns with you, in the unity
of the Holy Spirit, one God, for ever and ever.
Amen.   [BOOS, 144]

O God, you have so consecrated the covenant of marriage
that in it is represented the spiritual unity between Christ and
his Church: Send your blessing upon *N.* and *N.,* who come
to renew their promises to each other, and grant them your
grace, that they may so love, honor, and cherish each other in
faithfulness and patience, in wisdom and true godliness, that
their lives together may be a witness to your love and
forgiveness, and that their home may be a haven of blessing
and peace; through Jesus Christ our Lord, who lives and
reigns with you and the Holy Spirit, one God, now and for
ever. *Amen.*   [BOOS, 144]

Grant, O God, in your compassion, that *N.* and *N.,* having
taken each other in marriage, and affirming again the

covenant which they have made, may grow in forgiveness, loyalty, and love; and come at last to the eternal joys which you have promised through Jesus Christ our Lord; who lives and reigns with you, in the unity of the Holy Spirit, one God, for ever and ever. *Amen.*   [BOOS, 145]

In counseling

O Lord Jesus Christ, Who didst come to seek and to save that which was lost, and who hast committed to us the ministry of reconciliation, give me a discerning spirit to judge and advise aright. Grant that I may never make sad the hearts that thou wouldst not have saddened; nor, healing slightly the hurt of thy people, speak peace where there is no peace; but may faithfully and lovingly, firmly and considerately lead those who seek my help in the paths of truth and peace; for thy mercies' sake. *Amen.*   [PPB, NO. 199][50]

Before hearing a confession

Grant me, O Lord, the wisdom that sitteth at thy right hand, that I may judge thy people according to the right, and the poor with equity. Grant that I may so wield the keys of the Kingdom of Heaven, that I may open to none to whom it should be shut, nor shut it to any to whom it should be opened. Give purity to my intention, sincerity to my zeal, patience to my charity, and fruit to my labors. Grant that I may be mild, yet not remiss, stern, yet not cruel. Let me neither despise the poor nor flatter the rich. Give me gentleness to draw sinners unto thee, prudence in examination, wisdom in instruction. Grant me, I pray thee, skill to turn men aside from evil, perseverance to confirm them in good, zeal to persuade them to better things: give wisdom to my answers, rightness to my counsels: give me light in darkness, a good understanding in confusion, victory in difficulties. Let no vain conversations entangle me, nor evil defile me: let me save others and not myself be cast away. *Amen.* [MFP, 19]

O good Lord Jesus, who came to bear our sins, help me, a sinner, to be the minister of thy grace to this thy child; give me patience, wisdom, honesty and compassion, that I may hear and judge rightly in thy Name, who with the Father and the Holy Spirit, art God for ever and ever. *Amen.* [PPB, NO. 198][14]

Before sermons

Let the words of my mouth and the meditation of our hearts be always acceptable in your sight, O Lord, our strength and our redeemer. *Amen.* [PTL, 72][51]

Come, O Holy Spirit, come.
Come as the wind and cleanse;
come as the fire and burn;
convert and consecrate our lives
to our great good and your great glory;
through Jesus Christ our Lord.
Amen. [PTL, 73][52]

Take my lips, O Lord, and speak through them; take our minds and think with them. Take our hearts and set them on fire; through Jesus Christ our Lord. *Amen.* [PTL, 73][53]

Before worship

Almighty God, from whom every good prayer comes: Give us the spirit to praise you and thank you and call upon your Name, that our hearts may be warmed within us and our minds enlightened. Grant that we may worship you now in beauty, truth, and love; through Jesus Christ our Lord. *Amen.*   [PTL, 72][9]

Quiet our minds, O God, and gladden our hearts; that, as we come together to worship you, we may be open to your presence and find that this place is the very gate of heaven; through Jesus Christ our Lord. *Amen.*   [PTL, 72][54]

O Almighty God, who pours out on all who desire it the spirit of grace and of supplication: Deliver us, when we draw near to you, from coldness of heart and wanderings of mind, that with steadfast thoughts and kindled affections we may worship you in spirit and in truth; through Jesus Christ our Lord. *Amen.*   [833]

After worship

Grant, we beseech you, Almighty God, that the words which we have heard this day with our outward ears, may, through your grace, be so grafted inwardly in our hearts, that they may bring forth in us the fruit of good living, to the honor and praise of your Name; through Jesus Christ our Lord. *Amen.*   [834]

We thank you, Lord, for opening our ears to your Word and our eyes to your glory. We thank you for the good news of a redeemed creation and the vision of a new mankind. Send us forth in the power of your Spirit to live our lives in your world according to this revelation of your will; through Jesus Christ our Lord. *Amen.*   [PTL, 74][10]

VI
The Sick, Departed and Bereaved

The Sick, Departed and Bereaved

For the sick

O Father of mercies and God of all comfort, our only help in
time of need: We humbly beseech thee to behold, visit, and
relieve thy sick servant N. for whom our prayers are desired.
Look upon *him* with the eyes of thy mercy; comfort *him*
with a sense of thy goodness; preserve *him* from the
temptations of the enemy; and give *him* patience under *his*
affliction. In thy good time, restore *him* to health, and enable
him to lead the residue of *his* life in thy fear, and to thy glory;
and grant that finally *he* may dwell with thee in life
everlasting; through Jesus Christ our Lord. *Amen.* [458]

O God of heavenly powers, by the might of your command
you drive away from our bodies all sickness and all infirmity:
Be present in your goodness with your servant N., that *his*
weakness may be banished and *his* strength restored; and
that, *his* health being renewed, *he* may bless your holy
Name; through Jesus Christ our Lord. *Amen.* [458]

O God, the strength of the weak and the comfort of
sufferers: Mercifully accept our prayers, and grant to your
servant N. the help of your power, that *his* sickness may be
turned into health, and our sorrow into joy; through Jesus
Christ our Lord. *Amen.* [458]

Heavenly Father, giver of life and health: Comfort and relieve your sick servant *N.*, and give your power of healing to those who minister to *his* needs, that *he* may be strengthened in *his* weakness and have confidence in your loving care; through Jesus Christ our Lord. *Amen.*   [459]

O Almighty God, who art the giver of all health, and the aid of them that turn to thee for succor; We entreat thy strength and goodness in behalf of this thy servant, that *he* may be healed of *his* infirmities, to thine honor and glory; through Jesus Christ our Lord. *Amen.*   [28BCP, 315]

For a sick child

Lord Jesus Christ, Good Shepherd of the sheep, you gather the lambs in your arms and carry them in your bosom: We commend to your loving care this child *N.* Relieve *his* pain, guard *him* from all danger, restore to *him* your gifts of gladness and strength, and raise *him* up to a life of service to you. Hear us, we pray, for your dear Name's sake. *Amen.*   [459]

Heavenly Father, watch with us over your child *N.*, and grant that *he* may be restored to that perfect health which it is yours alone to give; through Jesus Christ our Lord. *Amen.*   [458]

O Lord Jesus Christ, Good Shepherd of the sheep, who dost gather the lambs with thine arms, and carry them in thy bosom: We commit into thy loving hands this child. Relieve *his* pain, guard *him* from all danger, restore unto *him* thy gifts of gladness and strength, and raise *him* up to a life of service to thee. Hear us, we beseech thee, for thy dear Name's sake. *Amen.*   [PPB, NO. 247][55]

For trust in God's healing

O God, the source of all health: So fill my heart with faith in your love, that with calm expectancy I may make room for your power to possess me, and gracefully accept your healing; through Jesus Christ our Lord. *Amen.* [461]

For sanctification of an illness

Sanctify, O Lord, the sickness of your servant N., that the sense of *his* weakness may add strength to *his* faith and seriousness to *his* repentance; and grant that *he* may live with you in everlasting life; through Jesus Christ our Lord. *Amen.* [460]

Anointing the sick

O blessed Redeemer, relieve, we beseech thee, by thy indwelling power, the distress of this thy servant; release *him* from sin, and drive away all pain of soul and body, that being restored to soundness of health, *he* may offer thee praise and thanksgiving; who livest and reignest with the Father and the Holy Ghost, one God, world without end. *Amen.*

As the Priest anoints the sick person on the forehead he says:

I anoint thee with oil, In the Name of the Father, and of the Son, and of the Holy Ghost; beseeching the mercy of our Lord Jesus Christ, that all thy pain and sickness of body being put to flight, the blessing of health may be restored unto thee. *Amen.* [MFP, 61]

or this

If the person is to be anointed, the Priest dips a thumb in the holy oil, and makes the sign of the cross on the sick person's forehead, saying

N., I anoint you with oil in the Name of the Father, and of the Son, and of the Holy Spirit. *Amen.*

The Priest may add

As you are outwardly anointed with this holy oil, so may our heavenly Father grant you the inward anointing of the Holy Spirit. Of his great mercy, may he forgive you your sins, release you from suffering, and restore you to wholeness and strength. May he deliver you from all evil, preserve you in all goodness, and bring you to everlasting life; through Jesus Christ our Lord. *Amen.*

In cases of necessity, a deacon or lay person may perform the anointing, using oil blessed by a bishop or priest. [456]

Laying on of hands for healing

N., I lay my hands upon you in the Name of the Father, and of the Son, and of the Holy Spirit, beseeching our Lord Jesus Christ to sustain you with his presence, to drive away all sickness of body and spirit, and to give you that victory of life and peace which will enable you to serve him both now and evermore. *Amen.*

or this

N., I lay my hands upon you in the Name of our Lord and Savior Jesus Christ, beseeching him to uphold you and fill you with his grace, that you may know the healing power of his love. *Amen.* [456]

For a convalescent

O Lord, whose compassions fail not, and whose mercies are new every morning: we give thee hearty thanks that it hath pleased thee to give to this our *brother* both relief from pain and hope of renewed health; continue, we beseech thee, in *him* the good work that thou hast begun; that, daily increasing in bodily strength, and humbly rejoicing in thy goodness, *he* may so order *his* life and conversation as always to think and do such things as shall please thee. Through Jesus Christ our Lord. *Amen.* [SAPB, 183]

For my recovery

O Lord Jesus Christ, who didst go about doing good and healing all manner of disease amongst the people, lay thy healing hand upon me, and if it be thy will restore me to my former health. May thy almighty strength support my weakness, and defend me from the enemy. May thy sustaining presence be with me to soothe each ache and pain.

O spare me a little, that I may recover my strength before I go hence and be no more seen. Heal me, O Lord, and I shall be healed. Save me, and I shall be saved, for thou art my strength.

Write, O Lord, thy sacred wounds on my heart that I may never forget them, and that in them I may read thy pains, that I may bear patiently every pain for thee. Write thy love on my heart that I may love only thee.

Lord, be merciful to me a sinner: Jesus, Son of the living God, have mercy upon me.

I commend my soul to God my Creator, who made me out of nothing: to Jesus Christ my Savior, who redeemed me with his precious Blood; to the Holy Ghost, who sanctified me in Baptism. Into thy hands, O Lord, I commend my spirit.

Let thy holy angels defend me from all powers of darkness. Let Mary, Mother of God, and all the blessed saints, pray for me a poor sinner.

> OUR FATHER.
>
> HAIL, MARY.
>
> GLORY BE.

Christ, when thou shalt call me hence,
Be thy Mother my defence,
Be thy Cross my victory.

Amen. [SAPB, 178]

171

When in pain

Lord Jesus Christ, by your patience in suffering you hallowed earthly pain and gave us the example of obedience to your Father's will: Be near me in my time of weakness and pain; sustain me by your grace, that my strength and courage may not fail; heal me according to your will; and help me always to believe that what happens to me here is of little account if you hold me in eternal life, my Lord and my God.
Amen.   [461]

In times of suffering

Lord God, whose blessed Son our Savior gave his body to be whipped and his face to be spit upon: Give us grace to accept joyfully the sufferings of the present time, confident of the glory that shall be revealed; through Jesus Christ your Son our Lord, who lives and reigns with you and the Holy Spirit, one God, for ever and ever. *Amen.*   [220]

For health of body and soul

May God the Father bless you, God the Son heal you, God the Holy Spirit give you strength. May God the holy and undivided Trinity guard your body, save your soul, and bring you safely to his heavenly country; where he lives and reigns for ever and ever. *Amen.*   [460]

For one who has had a heart attack

O God, giver of life and health, hope and courage, watch with this thy servant in *his* anxiety and helplessness. Bless those whom *he* loves and those who love *him*; guide those who minister to *him* in *his* weakness; give *him* patience and trust that *he* may be restored to serve thee with gladness; through Jesus Christ our Lord. *Amen.*   [PPB, NO. 243][14]

172

Before an operation

Almighty God our heavenly Father, we beseech thee graciously to comfort thy servant in *his* suffering, and to bless the means made use of for *his* cure. Fill *his* heart with confidence, that though *he* be sometime afraid, *he* yet may put *his* trust in thee; through Jesus Christ our Lord. *Amen.* [28BCP, 597]

Strengthen me, I beseech thee O God, to do what I have to do, to bear what I have to bear, that accepting thy healing gifts in the skill and patience of these doctors and nurses, I may be restored to usefulness in thy world with a thankful heart; through Jesus Christ our Lord. *Amen.* [PPB, NO. 252][14]

For an emergency baptism

In case of emergency, any baptized person may administer Baptism according to the following form. Using the given name of the one to be baptized (if known), pour water on him or her, saying

I baptize you in the Name of the Father, and of the Son, and of the Holy Spirit.

The Lord's Prayer is then said.
Other prayers, such as the following, may be added

Heavenly Father, we thank you that by water and the Holy Spirit you have bestowed upon this your servant the forgiveness of sin and have raised *him* to the new life of grace. Strengthen *him*, O Lord, with your presence, enfold *him* in the arms of your mercy, and keep *him* safe for ever.

The person who administers emergency Baptism should inform the priest of the appropriate parish, so that the fact can be properly registered.

If the baptized person recovers, the Baptism should be recognized at a public celebration of the Sacrament with a bishop or priest presiding, and the person baptized under emergency conditions, together with the sponsors or godparents, taking part in everything except the administration of the water. [313]

For faith in the resurrection

Lord Jesus Christ, by your death you took away the sting of death: Grant to us your servants so to follow in faith where you have led the way, that we may at length fall asleep peacefully in you and wake up in your likeness; for your tender mercies' sake. *Amen.* [504]

For a dying child

O Lord Jesus Christ, the only-begotten Son of God, who for our sakes didst become a babe in Bethlehem; we commit unto thy loving care this child whom thou art calling to thyself. Send thy holy angel to lead *him* gently to those heavenly habitations where the souls of them that sleep in thee have perpetual peace and joy, and hold *him* in the everlasting arms of thine unfailing love. Who livest and reignest, world without end. *Amen.* [SAPB, 194]

For a person near death

Almighty God, look on this your servant, lying in great weakness, and comfort *him* with the promise of life everlasting, given in the resurrection of your Son Jesus Christ our Lord. *Amen.* [462]

For one who is afraid to die

O Thou who art God from everlasting to everlasting, look with compassion on this thy child: Hold *him* in the arms of thy mercy and help *him* to know that *he* is safe in thy love; free *him* from fear, that *he* may repent and be saved, and restore *him* to fellowship with thee in *his* time and thine eternity; through Jesus Christ our Lord. *Amen.*
[PPB, NO. 261][14]

For the seemingly incurable

O Father of mercies, and God of all comfort, our only help in time of need; We fly unto thee for succor in behalf of this thy servant, here lying in great weakness of body. Look graciously upon *him*, O Lord; and the more the outward man decayeth, strengthen *him*, we beseech thee, so much the more continually with thy grace and Holy Spirit in the inner man. Give *him* unfeigned repentance for all the errors of *his* life past, and steadfast faith in thy Son Jesus; that *his* sins may be done away by thy mercy, and *his* pardon sealed in heaven; through the same thy Son, our Lord and Savior. *Amen.*   [28BCP, 316]

O Lord, who dost feel the pain of the world; look with mercy, we beseech thee, upon those who in their sickness and suffering are beyond the reach of human skill. To thee alone belongs the power of life, and these souls are thine. If in the mystery of thy providence it shall be their lot to bear their infirmity to the end, then, Lord, of thy love give them grace to endure bravely, and such an assurance of thy presence with them in it that they may, like their Savior, be made perfect through suffering. *Amen.*   [PPB, NO. 282][12]

For one who wants to die

O God, our Father, who hast made us for thyself, behold and bless this thy servant in *his* distress of mind and body; enfold *him* tenderly in the arms of thy mercy, give *him* patience to do thy will and, in thy good time, take *him* into thy holy keeping; through Jesus Christ our Lord. *Amen.*
[PPB, NO. 265][14]

For one dying outside the faith

O God, our Father, who in the Lord Jesus Christ came to seek and to save the wandering and the lost, we trust thee to deal graciously with this thy child; behold and bless those who love *him* and, if it be thy will, bring *him* home in thy good time to the ample house of thy love; through Jesus Christ our Savior. *Amen.* [PPB, NO. 262][14]

For all who suffer

Gracious God, the comfort of all who sorrow, the strength of all who suffer: Let the cry of those in misery and need come to you, that they may find your mercy present with them in all their afflictions; and give us, we pray, the strength to serve them for the sake of him who suffered for us, your Son Jesus Christ our Lord. *Amen.* [279]

For the victims of addiction

O blessed Lord, you ministered to all who came to you: Look with compassion upon all who through addiction have lost their health and freedom. Restore to them the assurance of your unfailing mercy; remove from them the fears that beset them; strengthen them in the work of their recovery; and to those who care for them, give patient understanding and persevering love. *Amen.* [831]

For the mentally ill

O heavenly Father, we beseech thee to have mercy upon all thy children who are living in mental darkness. Restore them to strength of mind and cheerfulness of spirit, and give them health and peace; through Jesus Christ our Lord. *Amen.* [28BCP, 598]

For a suicide

O God, who knowest all our lights and all our shadows, look with compassion on this thy child who has taken *his* life with *his* own hand and receive him as thine own. Deal graciously, we pray thee, with those who love *him*, and grant that in all their troubles they may know thy healing and redeeming love, made known to us in Jesus Christ our Lord. *Amen.* [PPB, NO. 301][14]

At the burial of an adult

O God, who by the glorious resurrection of your Son Jesus Christ destroyed death, and brought life and immortality to light: Grant that your servant N., being raised with him, may know the strength of his presence, and rejoice in his eternal glory; who with you and the Holy Spirit lives and reigns, one God, for ever and ever. *Amen.* [493]

O God, whose mercies cannot be numbered: Accept our prayers on behalf of your servant N., and grant *him* an entrance into the land of light and joy, in the fellowship of your saints; through Jesus Christ our Lord, who lives and reigns with you and the Holy Spirit, one God, now and for ever. *Amen.* [493]

At the burial of a child

O God, whose beloved Son took children into his arms and blessed them: Give us grace to entrust N., to your never-failing care and love, and bring us all to your heavenly kingdom; through Jesus Christ our Lord, who lives and reigns with you and the Holy Spirit, one God, now and for ever. *Amen.* [494]

For those who rest in Jesus

O Almighty God, the God of the spirits of all flesh, who by a voice from heaven didst proclaim, Blessed are the dead who die in the Lord: Multiply, we beseech thee, to those who rest in Jesus the manifold blessings of thy love, that the good work which thou didst begin in them may be made perfect unto the day of Jesus Christ. And of thy mercy, O heavenly Father, grant that we, who now serve thee on earth, may at last, together with them, be partakers of the inheritance of the saints in light; for the sake of thy Son Jesus Christ our Lord. *Amen.* [486]

For our beloved departed

And now, dear Lord, we give N. back to thee, who gavest *him* to us. Yet, as thou didst not lose *him* in giving, so we have not lost *him* forever by *his* return. For what is thine is always ours, if we are thine. And life is eternal; and love is immortal; and death is only an horizon; and an horizon is nothing save the limit of our sight. Lift us up, strong Son of God, that we may see further; cleanse our eyes that we may see more clearly; draw us closer to thyself, that we may know ourselves nearer to our beloved who are with thee; that where they are, and thou art, we too one day may be. *Amen.* [UNKNOWN]

Father of all, we pray to you for those we love, but see no longer: Grant them your peace; let light perpetual shine upon them; and, in your loving wisdom and almighty power, work in them the good purpose of your perfect will; through Jesus Christ our Lord. *Amen.* [504]

Into thy hands, O Lord, we commend thy servant *N.*, our dear *brother*, as into the hands of a faithful Creator and most merciful Savior, beseeching thee that *he* may be precious in thy sight. Wash *him*, we pray thee, in the blood of that immaculate Lamb that was slain to take away the sins of the world; that, whatsoever defilements *he* may have contracted in the midst of this earthly life being purged and done away, *he* may be presented pure and without spot before thee; through the merits of Jesus Christ thine only Son our Lord. *Amen.*   [488]

For departed parents

O God who didst command thy people, saying: Honor thy father and thy mother: of thy loving-kindness have mercy on the soul(s) of my *father* (and my mother) and forgive *them* all *their* sins; and I humbly pray thee that thou wouldest grant unto me to behold *their* face(s) in the glory of eternal felicity. Through Jesus Christ our Lord. *Amen.*   [SAPB, 196]

For all the faithful departed

O God, the King of saints, we praise and glorify your holy Name for all your servants who have finished their course in your faith and fear: for the blessed VirginMary; for the holy patriarchs, prophets, apostles, and martyrs; and for all your other righteous servants, known to us and unknown; and we pray that, encouraged by their examples, aided by their prayers, and strengthened by their fellowship, we also may be partakers of the inheritance of the saints in light; through the merits of your Son Jesus Christ our Lord. *Amen.*   [504]

A commendation at time of death

Depart, O Christian soul, out of this world;
In the name of God the Father Almighty who created you;
In the name of Jesus Christ who redeemed you;
In the name of the Holy spirit who sanctifies you.
May your rest be this day in peace,
    and your dwelling place in the Paradise of God.
Amen.   [464]

A commendatory prayer at death

Into your hands, O merciful Savior, we commend your
servant N. Acknowledge, we humbly beseech you, a sheep of
your own fold, a lamb of your own flock, a sinner of your
own redeeming. Receive *him* into the arms of your mercy,
into the blessed rest of everlasting peace, and into the
glorious company of the saints in light. *Amen.*

May *his* soul and the souls of all the departed, through the
mercy of God, rest in peace. *Amen.*   [465]

O Almighty God, with whom do live the spirits of just men
made perfect, after they are delivered from their earthly
prisons; We humbly commend the soul of this thy servant,
our dear *brother*, into thy hands, as into the hands of a
faithful Creator, and most merciful Savior; beseeching thee,
that it may be precious in thy sight. Wash it, we pray thee, in
the blood of that immaculate Lamb, that was slain to take
away the sins of the world; that whatsoever defilements it
may have contracted, through the lusts of the flesh or the
wiles of Satan, being purged and done away, it may be
presented pure and without spot before thee; through the
merits of Jesus Christ thine only Son our Lord.
Amen.   [28BCP, 317]

Prayers for a funeral vigil

Dear Friends: It was our Lord Jesus himself who said, "Come to me, all you who labor and are burdened, and I will give you rest." Let us pray, then, for our brother (sister) N., that *he* may rest from *his* labors, and enter into the light of God's eternal sabbath rest.

Receive, O Lord, your servant, for *he* returns to you.
Into your hands, O Lord, we commend our brother (sister) N.

Wash *him* in the holy font of everlasting life, and clothe *him* in *his* heavenly wedding garment.
Into your hands, O Lord, we commend our brother (sister) N.

May *he* hear your words of invitation, "Come, you blessed of my Father."
Into your hands, O Lord, we commend our brother (sister) N.

May *he* gaze upon you, Lord, face to face, and taste the blessedness of perfect rest.
Into your hands, O Lord, we commend our brother (sister) N.

May angels surround *him*, and saints welcome *him* in peace.
Into your hands, O Lord, we commend our brother (sister) N.

The Officiant concludes

Almighty God, our Father in heaven, before whom live all who die in the Lord: Receive our *brother N.* into the courts of your heavenly dwelling place. Let *his* heart and soul now ring out in joy to you, O Lord, the living God, and the God of those who live. This we ask through Christ our Lord. *Amen.*   [465]

Committal of the departed

In sure and certain hope of the resurrection to eternal life through our Lord Jesus Christ, we commend to Almighty God our *brother N.*, and we commit *his* body to the ground;* earth to earth, ashes to ashes, dust to dust. The

Lord bless *him* and keep *him*, the Lord make his face to shine upon *him* and be gracious to *him*, the Lord lift up his countenance upon *him* and give *him* peace. *Amen.* [501]

* *Or* the deep, *or* the elements, *or* its resting place.

For those bereaved

Grant, O Lord, to all who are bereaved the spirit of faith and courage, that they may have strength to meet the days to come with steadfastness and patience; not sorrowing as those without hope, but in thankful remembrance of your great goodness, and in the joyful expectation of eternal life with those they love. And this we ask in the Name of Jesus Christ our Savior. *Amen.* [505]

O God of grace and glory, we remember before you this day our brother (sister), N. We thank you for giving *him* to us, *his* family and friends, to know and to love as a companion on our earthly pilgrimage. In your boundless compassion, console us who mourn. Give us quiet confidence that we may continue our course in faith; through Jesus Christ our Lord. *Amen.* [BOOS, 157]

O merciful Father, you have taught us in your holy Word that you do not willingly afflict or grieve your children: Look with pity upon the sorrows of your servants for whom our prayers are offered. Remember them, O Lord, in mercy, nourish their souls with patience, comfort them with a sense of your goodness, lift up your countenance upon them, and give them peace; through Jesus Christ our Lord. *Amen.* [BOOS, 157]

Almighty God, Father of mercies and giver of comfort: Deal graciously, we pray, with all who mourn; that, casting all their care on you, they may know the consolation of your love; through Jesus Christ our Lord. *Amen.* [505]

For those bereaved by a sudden death

O God, our only help in time of need, watch with these thy people in their time of trouble; strengthen and quiet them with thy mercy, receive thy servant in *his* sudden death and take *him* into thy holy keeping; through Jesus Christ our Lord. *Amen.* [PPB, NO. 300][14]

For comfort in grief

Almighty God, we desire to acknowledge thee in all our ways and in all of the experiences that come to us in this life. We pray that thou wouldst lift us above the shadow and the sadness of this mortal life, into the light of thy comforting presence. Speak to us thy word of life as we stand in the presence of death; speak to us thy word of peace in the presence of separation and loneliness. Thou hast said, "In this world you shall have tribulation, but in me ye shall have peace." So, then, O God, we beseech thee to comfort us thy servants in our present sorrow and to give us a sure and certain confidence in thine abiding and unshakable peace. And this we ask in the Name of our Lord and Savior Jesus Christ. *Amen.* [UNKNOWN]

O Lord, we beseech thee, by all thy dealing with us, whether of joy or pain, of light or darkness, let us be brought to thee. Help us to value no treatment of thy grace simply because it makes us happy, or because it makes us sad; because it gives us or denies us what we want; but may all that you send to us bring us ever closer to thee; that knowing thy perfectness, we may be sure in all that comes to us in this life, that thou art still with us and with those we love, loving us, enlightening us, and giving us life eternal; through the strengthening and sustaining power of our Lord Jesus Christ. *Amen.* [UNKNOWN]

Most merciful God, whose wisdom is beyond our understanding, deal graciously with *N.N.* in *their* grief. Surround *them* with your love, that *they* may not be overwhelmed by *their* loss, but have confidence in your goodness, and strength to meet the days to come; through Jesus Christ our Lord. *Amen.*   [494]

O God, whose blessed Son on the cross did know the desolation of loneliness from thee; comfort these thy servants in their grief and emptiness, enfold them in the arms of thy mercy and give them peace; through Jesus Christ our Lord. *Amen.*   [PPB, NO. 318][14]

For one who has lost a child at birth

I give thanks unto thee, O Lord God, heavenly Father, through Jesus Christ, thy dear Son, that thou hast been so graciously present with me in all my needs, and even though the heavy burden of sorrow has come so soon upon me still thou dost grant me the comforting assurance that all things work together for good to them that love thee. O most merciful Father, I humbly offer thee my love and trust and tenderly commit the soul of my little one into thy keeping against the day when we shall be united in thy Presence; and I beseech thee, take not the comfort of thy Spirit from me, but grant me grace ever to learn and to do thy will; through Jesus Christ, thy Son, our Lord. *Amen.*   [PPB, NO. 296][56]

VII
Dedications, Blessings and Absolutions

Dedications, Blessings and Absolutions

At the dedication or founding of a Church

Dearly beloved in the Lord; forasmuch as devout and holy
men, as well under the Law as under the Gospel, moved
either by the express command of God, or by the secret
inspiration of the blessed Spirit, and acting agreeably to their
own reason and sense of the natural decency of things, have
erected houses for the public worship of God, and separated
them from all unhallowed, worldly, and common uses, in
order to fill men's minds with greater reverence for his
glorious Majesty, and affect their hearts with more devotion
and humility in his service; which pious works have been
approved of and graciously accepted by our heavenly Father;
Let us not doubt but that he will also favorably approve our
godly purpose of setting apart this place in solemn manner,
for the several Offices of religious worship, and let us
faithfully and devoutly beg his blessing on this our
undertaking. *Amen.*   [28BCP, 564]

O Eternal God, mighty in power, and of majesty
incomprehensible, whom the heaven of heavens cannot
contain, much less the walls of temples made with hands;
and who yet hast been graciously pleased to promise thy
especial presence, wherever two or three of thy faithful
servants shall assemble in thy Name, to offer up their praises
and supplications unto thee; Vouchsafe, O Lord, to be
present with us, who are here gathered together with all

humility and readiness of heart, to consecrate this place to the honor of thy great Name; separating it henceforth from all unhallowed, ordinary, and common uses; and dedicating it to thy service, for reading thy holy Word, for celebrating thy holy Sacraments, for offering to thy glorious Majesty the sacrifices of prayer and thanksgiving, for blessing thy people in thy Name, and for all other holy offices: accept, O Lord, this service at our hands, and bless it with such success as may tend most to thy glory, and the furtherance of our happiness both temporal and spiritual; through Jesus Christ our blessed Lord and Savior. *Amen.*   [28BCP, 564]

Through the ages, Almighty God has moved his people to build houses of prayer and praise, and to set apart places for the ministry of his holy Word and Sacraments. With gratitude for the building (*or* rebuilding, *or* adornment) of (*name of church*), we are now gathered to dedicate and consecrate it in God's Name.*Amen.*   [567]

Almighty God, we thank you for making us in your image, to share in the ordering of your world. Receive the work of our hands in this place, now to be set apart for your worship, the building up of the living, and the remembrance of the dead, to the praise and glory of your Name; through Jesus Christ our Lord. *Amen.*   [567]

O Lord God of Israel, the heavens cannot contain you, yet you are pleased to dwell in the midst of your people, and have moved us to set apart a space on which to build a house of prayer: Accept and bless the work which we have now begun, that it may be brought to completion, to the honor and glory of your holy Name; through Jesus Christ our Lord, who lives and reigns with you in the unity of the Holy Spirit, one God, for ever and ever. *Amen.*   [BOOS, 200]

Regard, O Lord, the supplications of thy servants, and grant that whosoever in this house shall be received by Baptism into the congregation of Christ's flock, may be sanctified by the Holy Ghost, and may continue Christ's faithful soldier and servant unto his life's end. *Amen.* [28BCP, 565]

Grant, O Lord, that they who at this place shall in their own persons renew the promises and vows of their Baptism, and be Confirmed by the Bishop, may receive such a measure of thy Holy Spirit, that they may grow in grace unto their life's end. *Amen.* [28BCP, 565]

Grant, O Lord, that whosoever shall receive in this place the blessed Sacrament of the Body and Blood of Christ, may come to that holy ordinance with faith, charity, and true repentance; and being filled with thy grace and heavenly benediction, may, to their great and endless comfort, obtain remission of their sins, and all other benefits of his passion. *Amen.* [28BCP, 565]

Grant, O Lord, that by thy holy Word which shall be read and preached in this place, and by thy Holy Spirit grafting it inwardly in the heart, the hearers thereof may both perceive and know what things they ought to do, and may have power and strength to fulfill the same. *Amen.* [28BCP, 566]

Grant, O Lord, that whosoever shall be joined together in this place in the holy estate of Matrimony, may faithfully perform and keep the vow and covenant betwixt them made, and may remain in perfect love together unto their life's end. *Amen.* [28BCP, 566]

Grant, we beseech thee, blessed Lord, that whosoever shall draw near to thee in this place, to give thee thanks for the benefits which they have received at thy hands, to set forth thy most worthy praise, to confess their sins unto thee, and to ask such things as are requisite and necessary, as well for the body as for the soul, may do it with such steadiness of faith, and with such seriousness, affection, and devotion of mind, that thou mayest accept their bounden duty and service and vouchsafe to give whatever in thy infinite wisdom thou shalt see to be most expedient for them. All which we beg for Jesus Christ's sake, our most blessed Lord and Savior. *Amen.*   [28BCP, 566]

O most glorious God, whom the heaven of heavens cannot contain; Graciously accept the Dedication of this place to thy service; and grant that all who shall call upon thee here may worship thee in spirit and in truth, and may in their lives show forth thy praise; through Jesus Christ our Lord. *Amen.*   [28BCP, 567]

Almighty God, all times are your seasons, and all occasions invite your tender mercies: Accept our prayers and intercessions offered in this place today and in the days to come; through Jesus Christ, our Medicator and Advocate. *Amen.*   [572]

We give you thanks, O God, for the gifts of your people, and for the work of many hands, which have beautified this place and furnished it for the celebration of your holy mysteries. Accept and bless all we have done, and grant that in these earthly things we may behold the order and beauty of things heavenly; through Jesus Christ our Lord. *Amen.*   [573]

At the laying of a cornerstone

Lord Jesus Christ, Son of the living God, you are the brightness of the Father's glory and the express image of his person, the one foundation and the chief cornerstone: Bless what we have now done in the laying of this stone. Be the beginning, the increase, and the consummation of this work undertaken to the glory of your Name; who with the Father and the Holy Spirit live and reign, one God, for ever and ever. *Amen.* [BOOS, 201]

For benefactors

We bless your Name, O Lord, because it has pleased you to enable your *servant N. (N.)* to offer *this gift* for your worship. Remember *him* for good, and grant that all who benefit from *this gift* may show their thankfulness to you by using *it* in accordance with your will; through Jesus Christ our Lord. *Amen.* [BOOS, 194]

Anniversary of the dedication of a church

Almighty God, to whose glory we celebrate the dedication of this house of prayer: We give you thanks for the fellowship of those who have worshiped in this place, and we pray that all who seek you here may find you, and be filled with your joy and peace; through Jesus Christ our Lord, who lives and reigns with you, in the unity of the Holy Spirit, one God, now and for ever. *Amen.* [254]

For the dedication of church furnishings

O God, whose blessed Son has sanctified and transfigured the use of material things: Receive *this* _____ which we offer, and grant that *it* may proclaim your love, benefit your Church, and minister grace and joy to those who use *it*; through Jesus Christ our Lord. *Amen.* [BOOS, 192]

Almighty God, we thank you that you have put it into the hearts of your people to make offerings for your service, and have been pleased to accept their gifts. Be with us now and bless us as we set apart *this* _____ to your praise and glory [and in memory (honor) of _____]; through Jesus Christ our Lord. *Amen.*   [BOOS, 193]

Dedication of liturgical vestments

O God, you revealed your Son clothed in majesty and glory: Accept *this* _____ for the use of the *clergy* of your Church, that, being clothed with humility as they minister to you, they may show forth his eternal splendor; through Jesus Christ our Lord. *Amen.*   [BOOS, 191]

Dedication of surplices and albs

O God, before whose heavenly throne your servants minister to you, clothed in white robes: Accept *this* _____ which we dedicate for the use of the *ministers* of your Church, that serving before your earthly throne, they may worship you in spirit and in truth; through Jesus Christ our Lord. *Amen.*   [BOOS, 190]

Dedication of a funeral pall

O God, who baptized us into the Body of your Son Jesus Christ, and made us members with different functions, all necessary and all to be honored: Make this pall a sign of our common membership in Christ, that we may know those who have departed this earthly life, not as the world esteems them, but as you know and love them; through Jesus Christ our Lord. *Amen.*   [BOOS, 192]

Dedication of a vessel for incense

Almighty God, whose only-begotten Son received from the wise men a gift of incense and made for us the pure oblation foretold by the prophet: We dedicate to your worship *this vessel*, that our prayers may ascend in your sight as the incense, and the pure oblation of our Lord be proclaimed from farthest east to farthest west; through Jesus Christ our Lord. *Amen.*   [BOOS, 190]

Dedication of an organ or musical instrument

O Lord, before whose throne trumpets sound, and saints and angels sing the songs of Moses and the Lamb: Accept *this organ* for the worship of your temple, that with the voice of music we may proclaim your praise and tell it abroad; through Jesus Christ our Lord. *Amen.*   [BOOS, 189]

Dedication of a Bible, lectionary, or gospel book

O heavenly Father, whose blessed Son taught the disciples in all the Scriptures the things concerning himself: Accept this _____ which we dedicate here today, and grant that we may so diligently search your holy Word that we may find in it the wisdom that leads to salvation; through Jesus Christ our Lord. *Amen.*   [BOOS, 185]

Dedication of a repository for the Scriptures

Almighty God, who declared your will to the prophets and sages of Israel, and revealed your glory in the Word made flesh: Accept, we pray, this repository for the Holy Scriptures, and grant that through prayer and worship we may know you as you speak to us today; through Jesus Christ our Lord. *Amen.*   [BOOS, 185]

Dedication of a pulpit-lectern

Almighty God, in every age you have spoken through the voices of prophets, pastors, and teachers: Purify the lives and lips of those who read and proclaim your holy Word from *this ambo* which we dedicate today, that your word only may be proclaimed, and your word only may be heard; through Jesus Christ our Lord. *Amen.*   [BOOS, 187]

Dedication of chairs, benches and prayer desks

O Lord God Almighty, you disclosed in a vision the elders seated around your throne: Accept *this chair* for the use of those called to minister in your earthly sanctuary, and grant that those who serve you here may do so with reverence and love, to your honor and glory; through Jesus Christ our Lord. *Amen.*   [BOOS, 188]

Dedication of altar cloths and hangings

O glorious God, all your works proclaim your perfect beauty: Accept our offering of this _____ , and grant that it may adorn this sanctuary and show forth your glory; through Jesus Christ our Lord. *Amen.*   [BOOS, 184]

Dedication of a bell

O God, accept our offering of this bell, which we consecrate today (and to which we give the name _____): Grant that in this generation and in those that are to come, its voice may continually call your people to praise and worship; through Jesus Christ our Lord. *Amen.*   [BOOS, 182]

Dedication of a service book

Bless us, O Lord of hosts, as we use this _____ which we dedicate to your service, and grant that as your saints and angels always serve you in heaven, so we may worship you acceptably on earth; through Jesus Christ our Lord. *Amen.* [BOOS, 184]

Dedication of pictures and statues

Almighty God, whose Son our Savior manifested your glory in his flesh, and sanctified the outward and visible to be a means to perceive realities unseen: Accept, we pray, this representation of _____ ; and grant that as we look upon it, our hearts may be drawn to things which can be seen only by the eye of faith; through Jesus Christ our Lord. *Amen.* [BOOS, 189]

Dedication of a stained glass window

O Lord God, the whole world is filled with the radiance of your glory: Accept our offering of this window which we now dedicate to you for the adornment of this place and the inspiration of your people. Grant that as the light shines through it in many colors, so our lives may show forth the beauty of your manifold gifts of grace; through Jesus Christ our Lord. *Amen.* [BOOS, 188]

Dedication of chalices and patens

Almighty God, whose blessed Son instituted the Sacrament of his Body and Blood: Grant that all who receive the holy Mysteries from *these vessels*, which we now consecrate for use in your Church, may be sustained by his presence and enjoy for ever his heavenly benediction; who lives and reigns in glory everlasting. *Amen.* [BOOS, 182]

Dedication of an aumbry for the Sacrament

O Lord God, Father of our Savior Jesus Christ, who before
his passion instituted the Sacrament of his Body and Blood:
Grant that in *this aumbry (tabernacle)* which we set apart
today, the outward signs of his covenant may be kept in
safety, and that we may show forth his death and
resurrection until he comes in glory; who lives and reigns for
ever and ever. *Amen.*   [BOOS, 186]

Dedication of a cross

O gracious God, who in your mercy ordained that your Son
should suffer death on a cross of shame: We thank you that it
has become for us the sign of his triumph and the banner of
our salvation; and we pray that *this cross* may draw our
hearts to him, who leads us to the glory of your kingdom;
where you live and reign for ever and ever.
Amen.   [BOOS, 183]

Dedication of an aumbry for oils

O Lord God of hosts, who commanded priests of the Old
Covenant to set apart oil for the anointing of kings and
priests, and by your Apostle James commanded the
presbyters of your Church to anoint the sick: We here offer
to you *this aumbry* for the safe-keeping of the oils set apart
for the anointing of baptism and for the ministry of healing;
through him who was anointed as the Christ, and who lives
and reigns for ever and ever. *Amen.*   [BOOS, 186]

Dedication of candlesticks and lamps

O heavenly Father, who revealed to us the vision of your Son
in the midst of the candlesticks, and of your Spirit in seven
lamps of fire before your throne: Grant that *these lights*

(*lamps*), to be kindled for your glory, may be to us a sign of your presence and the promise of eternal light; through Jesus Christ our Lord. *Amen.*   [BOOS, 183]

Maundy Thursday agape blessing over wine

Blessed are you, O Lord our God, King of the universe. You create the fruit of the vine; and on this night you have refreshed us with the cup of salvation in the Blood of your Son Jesus Christ. Glory to you for ever and ever. *Amen.*   [BOOS, 93]

Maundy Thursday agape blessing over bread

Blessed are you, O Lord our God, King of the universe. You bring forth bread from the earth; and on this night you have given us the bread of life in the Body of your Son Jesus Christ. As grain scattered upon the earth is gathered into one loaf, so gather your Church in every place into the kingdom of your Son. To you be glory and power for ever and ever. *Amen.*   [BOOS, 94]

Maundy Thursday agape blessing over other foods

Blessed are you, O Lord our God, King of the universe. You have blessed the earth to bring forth food to satisfy our hunger. Let this food strengthen us in the fast that is before us, that following our Savior in the way of the cross, we may come to the joy of his resurrection. For yours is the kingdom and the power and the glory, now and for ever. *Amen.*   [BOOS, 94]

Easter household blessing over lamb

Stir up our memory, O Lord, as we eat this Easter lamb that, remembering Israel of old, who in obedience to your command ate the Paschal lamb and was delivered from the bondage of slavery, we, your new Israel, may rejoice in the resurrection of Jesus Christ, the true Lamb who has delivered us from the bondage of sin and death, and who lives and reigns for ever and ever. *Amen.*   [BOOS, 96]

Easter household blessing over bread

Blessed are you, O Lord our God; you bring forth bread from the earth and make the risen Lord to be for us the Bread of life: Grant that we who daily seek the bread which sustains our bodies may also hunger for the food of everlasting life, Jesus Christ our Lord. *Amen.*   [BOOS, 95]

Easter household blessing over wine

Blessed are you, O Lord our God, creator of the fruit of the vine: Grant that we who share this wine, which gladdens our hearts, may share for ever and new life of the true Vine, your Son Jesus Christ our Lord. *Amen.*   [BOOS, 95]

Easter household blessing over eggs

O Lord our God, in celebration of the Paschal feast we have prepared these eggs from your creation: Grant that they may be to us a sign of the new life and immortality promised to those who follow your Son, Jesus Christ our Lord. *Amen.*   [BOOS, 96]

Easter household blessing over other foods

Blessed are you, O Lord our God; you have given us the risen Savior to be the Shepherd of your people: Lead us, by him, to springs of living waters, and feed us with the food that endures to eternal life; where with you, O Father, and with the Holy Spirit, he lives and reigns, one God, for ever and ever. *Amen.* [BOOS, 96]

Grace at meals

Give us grateful hearts, our Father, for all your mercies, and make us mindful of the needs of others; through Jesus Christ our Lord. *Amen.* [835]

Bless, O Lord, your gifts to our use and us to your service; for Christ's sake. *Amen.* [835]

Blessed are you, O Lord God, King of the Universe, for you give us food to sustain our lives and make our hearts glad; through Jesus Christ our Lord. *Amen.* [835]

For these and all his mercies, God's holy Name be blessed and praised; through Jesus Christ our Lord. *Amen.* [835]

Grant, O Lord, that our fellowship may be the revelation of your presence, and turn our daily bread into bread of life; through Jesus Christ our Lord. *Amen.* [PTL, 75][57]

The eyes of all wait upon you, O Lord: and you give them their food in due season. You open wide your hand, and satisfy the needs of every living creature. Glory to the Father, and to the Son, and to the Holy Spirit: as in the beginning, so now, and for ever. *Amen.* [PTL, 76][58]

Be present at our table, Lord;
Be here and everywhere adored.
Thy creatures bless, and grant that we
May feast in Paradise with thee.
Amen. [PTL, 76][59]

General pronouncements of blessing

The Lord bless you and keep you. *Amen.*

The Lord make his face to shine upon you and be gracious to you. *Amen.*

The Lord lift up his countenance upon you and give you peace. *Amen.*   [114]

The peace of God, which passeth all understanding, keep your hearts and minds in the knowledge and love of God, and of his Son Jesus Christ our Lord; and the blessing of God Almighty, the Father, the Son, and the Holy Ghost, be amongst you, and remain with you always. *Amen.*   [339]

The blessing of God Almighty, the Father, the Son, and the Holy Spirit, be upon you and remain with you for ever. *Amen.*   [339]

Unto God's gracious mercy and protection we commit you. The Lord bless you and keep you. The Lord make his face to shine upon you, and be gracious unto you. The Lord lift up his countenance upon you, and give you peace, both now and evermore. *Amen.*   [28BCP, 332]

The God of peace, who brought again from the dead our Lord Jesus Christ, the great Shepherd of the sheep, through the blood of the everlasting covenant: Make you perfect in every good work to do his will, working in you that which is well-pleasing in his sight; through Jesus Christ, to whom be glory for ever and ever. *Amen.*   [503]

May Almighty God, the Father, the Son, and the Holy Ghost, bless you and keep you, now and for evermore. *Amen.*   [28BCP, 342]

The blessing, mercy, and grace of God Almighty, the Father, the Son, and the Holy Spirit, be upon you, and remain with you for ever. *Amen.*   [523]

May God the Father, who by Baptism adopts us as his children, grant you grace. *Amen.*

May God the Son, who sanctified a home at Nazareth, fill you with love. *Amen.*

May God the Holy Spirit, who has made the Church one family, keep you in peace. *Amen.*   [445]

Blessing to be used by a deacon or lay person

The Lord bless us, and keep us. The Lord make his face to shine upon us, and be gracious unto us. The Lord lift up his countenance upon us, and give us peace, both now and evermore. *Amen.*   [28BCP, 63]

The almighty and merciful Lord, Father, Son, and Holy Spirit, bless us and keep us. *Amen.*   [140]

Advent seasonal blessings

May Almighty God, by whose providence our Savior Christ came among us in great humility, sanctify you with the light of his blessing and set you free from all sin. *Amen.*

May he whose second Coming in power and great glory we await, make you steadfast in faith, joyful in hope, and constant in love. *Amen.*

May you, who rejoice in the first Advent of our Redeemer, at his second Advent be rewarded with unending life. *Amen.*

And the blessing of God Almighty, the Father, the Son, and the Holy Spirit, be upon you and remain with you for ever. *Amen.*   [BOOS, 20]

May the Sun of Righteousness shine upon you and scatter the darkness from before your path; and the blessing of God Almighty, the Father, the Son, and the Holy Spirit, be among you, and remain with you always. *Amen.* [BOOS, 21]

Christmas seasonal blessings

May Almighty God, who sent his Son to take our nature upon him, bless you in this holy season, scatter the darkness of sin, and brighten your heart with the light of his holiness. *Amen.*

May God, who sent his angels to proclaim the glad news of the Savior's birth, fill you with joy, and make you heralds of the Gospel. *Amen.*

May God, who in the Word made flesh joined heaven to earth and earth to heaven, give you his peace and favor. *Amen.*

And the blessing of God Almighty, the Father, the Son, and the Holy Spirit, be upon you and remain with you for ever. *Amen.* [BOOS, 21]

May Christ, who by his Incarnation gathered into one things earthly and heavenly, fill you with his joy and peace; and the blessing of God Almighty, the Father, the Son, and the Holy Spirit, be among you, and remain with you always. *Amen.* [BOOS, 21]

Epiphany seasonal blessings

May Almighty God, who led the Wise Men by the shining of a star to find the Christ, the Light from Light, lead you also, in your pilgrimage, to find the Lord. *Amen.*

May God, who sent the Holy Spirit to rest upon the Only-begotten at his baptism in the Jordan River, pour out that Spirit on you who have come to the waters of new birth. *Amen.*

May God, by the power that turned water into wine at the wedding feast at Cana, transform your lives and make glad your hearts. *Amen.*

And the blessing of God Almighty, the Father, the Son, and the Holy Spirit, be upon you and remain with you for ever. *Amen.*   [BOOS, 22]

May Christ, the Son of God, be manifest in you, that your lives may be a light to the world; and the blessing of God Almighty, the Father, the Son, and the Holy Spirit, be among you, and remain with you always. *Amen.*   [BOOS, 22]

Easter seasonal blessings

May Almighty God, who has redeemed us and made us his children through the resurrection of his Son our Lord, bestow upon you the riches of his blessing. *Amen.*

May God, who through the water of baptism has raised us from sin into newness of life, make you holy and worthy to be united with Christ for ever. *Amen.*

May God, who has brought us out of bondage to sin into true and lasting freedom in the Redeemer, bring you to your eternal inheritance. *Amen.*

And the blessing of God Almighty, the Father, the Son, and the Holy Spirit, be upon you and remain with you for ever. *Amen.*   [BOOS, 24]

The God of peace, who brought again from the dead our Lord Jesus Christ, the great Shepherd of the sheep, through the blood of the everlasting covenant, make you perfect in every good work to do his will, working in you that which is well-pleasing in his sight; and the blessing of God Almighty, the Father, the Son, and the Holy Spirit, be among you, and remain with you always. *Amen.* [boos, 25]

Pentecost seasonal blessings

May Almighty God, who enlightened the minds of the disciples by pouring out upon them the Holy Spirit, make you rich with his blessing, that you may abound more and more in that Spirit for ever. *Amen.*

May God, who sent the Holy Spirit as a flame of fire that rested upon the heads of the disciples, burn out all evil from your hearts, and make them shine with the pure light of his presence. *Amen.*

May God, who by the Holy Spirit caused those of many tongues to proclaim Jesus as Lord, strengthen your faith and send you out to bear witness to him in word and deed. *Amen.*

And the blessing of God Almighty, the Father, the Son, and the Holy Spirit, be upon you and remain with you for ever. *Amen.* [boos, 25]

May the Spirit of truth lead you into all truth, giving you grace to confess that Jesus Christ is Lord, and to proclaim the wonderful works of God; and the blessing of God Almighty, the Father, the Son, and the Holy Spirit, be among you, and remain with you always. *Amen.* [boos, 25]

Trinity Sunday blessings

The Lord bless you and keep you. *Amen.*

The Lord make his face to shine upon you, and be gracious to you. *Amen.*

The Lord lift up his countenance upon you, and give you peace. *Amen.*

The Lord God Almighty, Father, Son, and Holy Spirit, the holy and undivided Trinity, guard you, save you, and bring you to that heavenly City, where he lives and reigns for ever and ever. *Amen.* [BOOS, 26]

May God the Holy Trinity make you strong in faith and love, defend you on every side, and guide you in truth and peace; and the blessing of God Almighty, the Father, the Son, and the Holy Spirit, be among you, and remain with you always. *Amen.* [BOOS, 26]

All Saints blessings

May Almighty God, to whose glory we celebrate this festival of all the Saints, be now and evermore your guide and companion in the way. *Amen.*

May God, who has bound us together in the company of the elect, in this age and the age to come, attend to the prayers of his faithful servants on your behalf, as he hears your prayers for them. *Amen.*

May God, who has given us, in the lives of his saints, patterns of holy living and victorious dying, strengthen your faith and devotion, and enable you to bear witness to the truth against all adversity. *Amen.*

And the blessing of God Almighty, the Father, the Son, and the Holy Spirit, be upon you and remain with you for ever. *Amen.* [BOOS, 26]

The preceding blessing may be adapted for use at a Patronal Festival.

May God give you grace to follow his saints in faith and hope and love; and the blessing of God Almighty, the Father, the Son, and the Holy Spirit, be among you, and remain with you always. *Amen.*   [BOOS, 27]

For consecration of chrism

Eternal Father, whose blessed Son was anointed by the Holy Spirit to be the Savior and servant of all, we pray you to consecrate this oil, that those who are sealed with it may share in the royal priesthood of Jesus Christ; who lives and reigns with you and the Holy Spirit, for ever and ever. *Amen.*   [BOOS, 209]

For consecration of a grave

O God, whose blessed Son was laid in a sepulcher in the garden: Bless, we pray, this grave, and grant that *he* whose body is (is to be) buried here may dwell with Christ in paradise, and may come to your heavenly kingdom; through your Son Jesus Christ our Lord. *Amen.*   [503]

For the blessing of a home

Visit, O blessed Lord, this home with the gladness of your presence. Bless *all* who *live* here with the gift of your love; and grant that *they* may manifest your love (to each other and) to all whose lives *they touch.* May *they* grow in grace and in the knowledge and love of you; guide, comfort, and strengthen *them*; and preserve *them* in peace, O Jesus Christ, now and for ever. *Amen.*   [BOOS, 140]

O Lord God Almighty, bless this place (*or* this house) that here may abide health, purity, victory, strength, humility, goodness, meekness, fulfillment of the law, and giving of thanks to God the Father, the Son, and the Holy Ghost; and let thy blessing remain on this place (*or* this house) and on all who shall dwell here, now and evermore. *Amen.*   [MFP, 177]

For the blessing of an airplane

O God, who hast made all things for thyself, and hast appointed every element of this world for the service of men; bless, we beseech thee, this airplane; that every evil and danger being done away, it may serve to make the praise and glory of thy holy Name more widely known, and the temporal affairs of men to be more speedily carried on; and grant that the minds of those who fly therein may cherish the desire for heavenly things. Through Christ our Lord. *Amen.* [MFP, 202]

For the blessing of a car

Assist us mercifully O Lord in these our supplications and prayers, and vouchsafe to bless this car: give thy holy Angels charge concerning it, that all who shall ride therein may be saved and protected from every danger. As by thy deacon Philip thou didst give faith and grace unto the Ethiopian eunuch as he sat in his chariot and read thy sacred law, so now unto thy servants show the way of salvation; that those who by the help of thy grace are ever intent upon good works, may through all the changes and chances of this mortal life be made worthy to obtain eternal joys. Through Christ our Lord. *Amen.* [MFP, 203]

For the blessing of a boat

Be favorable O Lord, unto our prayers, and with thy right hand bless this boat and all who shall voyage therein; stretch forth unto them thy holy arm to be their protection as thou

didst stretch it forth unto blessed Peter when he walked upon
the sea; and do thou send thy holy Angel from heaven to
keep and deliver this vessel from every peril, together with
those who voyage therein: and graciously behold thy
servants, that all perils being done away, they may by a
favorable course come to a fair haven; and their business
ended, return rejoicing to their own homes. Who livest and
reignest God, world without end. *Amen.*   [MFP, 204]

For the blessing of palms

It is right to praise you, Almighty God, for the acts of love by
which you have redeemed us through your Son Jesus Christ
our Lord. On this day he entered the holy city of Jerusalem in
triumph, and was proclaimed as King of kings by those who
spread their garments and branches of palm along his way.
Let these branches be for us signs of his victory, and grant
that we who bear them in his name may ever hail him as our
King, and follow him in the way that leads to eternal life;
who lives and reigns in glory with you and the Holy Spirit,
now and for ever. *Amen.*   [271]

Bless, O Lord, we beseech thee, these branches of the palm
tree: and grant that what thy people today show forth
corporally for thy honor, they may perform spiritually with
great devotion; and by ardently loving good works, may at
last gain the victory over their enemy. Through thy Son Jesus
Christ our Lord, who with thee, in the unity of the Holy
Spirit, liveth and reigneth God, world without end.
Amen.   [MFP, 223]

For the blessing of ashes

O God, who desirest not the death of a sinner, but rather that
he should turn from his sin and be saved: mercifully look

upon the frailty of our mortal nature, and of thy goodness vouchsafe to bless these ashes now to be set upon our heads in token of humility and to obtain thy pardon; that we, knowing we are but dust, and that for our unworthiness unto dust shall we return, may through thy mercy be found meet to receive forgiveness of all our sins, and those good things which thou hast promised to the penitent. Through Christ our Lord. *Amen.* [MFP, 221]

Almighty God, you have created us out of the dust of the earth: Grant that these ashes may be to us a sign of our mortality and penitence, that we may remember that it is only by your gracious gift that we are given everlasting life; through Jesus Christ our Savior. *Amen.* [265]

For the blessing of a space craft

O God, the King and Lord of all, who hast created all things in the universe: graciously hear our prayers, and bless this craft now prepared for the journeys of thy servants in space. Be present with those who are charged with its navigation, protect them in all perils; prosper them in their course, and bring them to their destination; and at length conduct them in safety to the haven where they would be. Through thy Son, Jesus Christ our Lord, who with thee, in the unity of the Holy Spirit, liveth and reigneth God, world without end. *Amen.* [MFP, 253]

For the blessing of a home for dispossessed children

Almighty God, our heavenly Father, whose blessed Son did share at Nazareth the life of an earthly home: Bless, we beseech thee, the home of these children; and grant wisdom and understanding to all who have the care of them, that they may grow up in thy constant respect and love; through thy Son Jesus Christ our Lord. *Amen.* [MFP, 271]

For the blessing of oil for anointing

O Lord, holy Father, giver of health and salvation: Send your
Holy Spirit to sanctify this oil; that, as your holy apostles
anointed many that were sick and healed them, so may those
who in faith and repentance receive this holy unction be
made whole; through Jesus Christ our Lord, who lives and
reigns with you and the Holy Spirit, one God, for ever and
ever. *Amen.*   [455]

For restoring of things profaned

Almighty God, by the radiance of your Son's appearing you
have purified a world corrupted by sin: We humbly pray that
you would continue to be our strong defense against the
attacks of our enemies; and grant that (this _____ , and)
whatsoever in this *church* has been stained or defiled through
the craft of Satan or by human malice, may be purified and
cleansed by your abiding grace; that this place, purged from
all pollution, may be restored and sanctified, to the glory of
your Name; through Jesus Christ our Lord, who lives and
reigns with you and the Holy Spirit, one God, now and for
ever. *Amen.*   [BOOS, 203]

At the secularizing of a consecrated building

Lord God, in your great goodness you once accepted to your
honor and glory this building, now secularized: Receive our
praise and thanksgiving for the blessings, help, and comfort
which you bestowed upon your people in this place.
Continue, we pray, your many mercies in your Church, that
we may be conscious at all times of your unchanging love;
through Jesus Christ our Lord. *Amen.*   [BOOS, 206]

Assist us mercifully, O Lord, in these our prayers, and dispose the way of your servants towards the attainment of everlasting salvation; that among the swift and varied changes of this world, our hearts may surely there be fixed where true joys are to be found; through Jesus Christ our Lord. *Amen.* [BOOS, 206]

The Lord bless us and keep us. *Amen.*
The Lord make his face to shine upon us,
    and be gracious to us. *Amen.*
The Lord lift up his countenance upon us,
    and give us peace. *Amen.* [BOOS, 206]

Declarations of absolution

Almighty God, our heavenly Father, who of his great mercy hath promised forgiveness of sins to all those who with hearty repentance and true faith turn unto him, have mercy upon you, pardon and deliver you from all your sins, confirm and strengthen you in all goodness, and bring you to everlasting life; through Jesus Christ our Lord. *Amen.* [332]

Almighty God have mercy on you, forgive you all your sins through our Lord Jesus Christ, strengthen you in all goodness, and by the power of the Holy Spirit keep you in eternal life. *Amen.* [455]

Our Lord Jesus Christ, who offered himself to be sacrificed for us to the Father, and who conferred power on his Church to forgive sins, absolve you through my ministry by the grace of the Holy Spirit, and restore you in the perfect peace of the Church. *Amen.* [451]

Almighty God, the Father of our Lord Jesus Christ, who desireth not the death of a sinner, but rather that he may turn from his wickedness and live, hath given power, and commandment, to his Ministers, to declare and pronounce to his people, being penitent, the Absolution and Remission of their sins. He pardoneth and absolveth all those who truly repent, and unfeignedly believe his holy Gospel.

Wherefore let us beseech him to grant us true repentance, and his Holy Spirit, that those things may please him which we do at this present; and that the rest of our life hereafter may be pure and holy; so that at the last we may come to his eternal joy; through Jesus Christ our Lord. *Amen.* [28BCP, 7]

Our Lord Jesus Christ, who has left power to his Church to absolve all sinners who truly repent and believe in him, of his great mercy forgive you all your offenses; and by his authority committed to me, I absolve you from all your sins: In the Name of the Father, and of the Son, and of the Holy Spirit. *Amen.* [451]

Our Lord Jesus Christ, who has left power to his Church to absolve all sinners who truly repent and believe in him, of his great mercy forgive you all your offenses; and by his authority committed to me, I absolve you from all your sins: In the Name of the Father, and of the Son, and of the Holy Spirit. *Amen.* [448]

Almighty God have mercy on you, forgive you all your sins through our Lord Jesus Christ, strengthen you in all goodness, and by the power of the Holy Spirit keep you in eternal life. *Amen.* [117]

A deacon or lay person using the preceding form remains kneeling, and substitutes "us" for "you" and "our" for "your."

The Almighty and merciful Lord grant you absolution and remission of all your sins, true repentance, amendment of life, and the grace and consolation of his Holy Spirit. *Amen.* [63]

A deacon or lay person using the preceding form remains kneeling, and substitutes "us" for "you" and "our" for "your."

Declaration of forgiveness
To be used by a deacon or lay person

(Also, see notations following two preceding absolutions)

Our Lord Jesus Christ, who offered himself to be sacrificed for us to the Father, forgives your sins by the grace of the Holy Spirit. *Amen.* [448]

VIII
Saints and Seasons

Saints and Seasons

Saint Andrew   *November 30*

Almighty God, who gave such grace to your apostle Andrew
that he readily obeyed the call of your Son Jesus Christ, and
brought his brother with him: Give us, who are called by
your Holy Word, grace to follow him without delay, and to
bring those near to us into his gracious presence; who lives
and reigns with you and the Holy Spirit, one God, now and
for ever. *Amen.*   [237]

Saint Barnabas   *June 11*

Grant, O God, that we may follow the example of your
faithful servant Barnabas, who, seeking not his own renown
but the well-being of your Church, gave generously of his life
and substance for the relief of the poor and the spread of the
Gospel; through Jesus Christ our Lord, who lives and reigns
with you and the Holy Spirit, one God, for ever and ever.
Amen.   [241]

Saint Bartholomew   *August 24*

Almighty and everlasting God, who gave to your apostle
Bartholomew grace truly to believe and to preach your
Word: Grant that your Church may love what he believed
and preach what he taught; through Jesus Christ our Lord,
who lives and reigns with you and the Holy Spirit, one God,
for ever and ever. *Amen.*   [243]

Saint James *July 25*

O gracious God, we remember before you today your servant and apostle James, first among the Twelve to suffer martyrdom for the Name of Jesus Christ; and we pray that you will pour out upon the leaders of your Church that spirit of self-denying service by which alone they may have true authority among your people; through Jesus Christ our Lord, who lives and reigns with you and the Holy Spirit, one God, now and for ever. *Amen.* [242]

Saint James of Jerusalem *October 23*

Grant, O God, that, following the example of your servant James the Just, brother of our Lord, your Church may give itself continually to prayer and to the reconciliation of all who are at variance and enmity; through Jesus Christ our Lord, who lives and reigns with you and the Holy Spirit, one God, now and for ever. *Amen.* [245]

Saint John *December 27*

Shed upon your Church, O Lord, the brightness of your light, that we, being illumined by the teaching of your apostle and evangelist John, may so walk in the light of your truth, that at length we may attain to the fullness of eternal life; through Jesus Christ our Lord, who lives and reigns with you and the Holy Spirit, one God, for ever and ever. *Amen.* [238]

Saint John the Baptist *June 24*

Almighty God, by whose providence your servant John the Baptist was wonderfully born, and sent to prepare the way of your Son our Savior by preaching repentance: Make us so to follow his teaching and holy life, that we may truly repent according to his preaching; and, following his example, constantly speak the truth, boldly rebuke vice, and patiently suffer for the truth's sake; through Jesus Christ your Son our Lord, who lives and reigns with you and the Holy Spirit, one God, for ever and ever. *Amen.*   [241]

Saint Joseph   *March 19*

O God, who from the family of your servant David raised up Joseph to be the guardian of your incarnate Son and the spouse of his virgin mother: Give us grace to imitate his uprightness of life and his obedience to your commands; through Jesus Christ our Lord, who lives and reigns with you and the Holy Spirit, one God, for ever and ever. *Amen.*   [239]

Saint Luke   *October 18*

Almighty God, who inspired your servant Luke the physician to set forth in the Gospel the love and healing power of your Son: Graciously continue in your Church this love and power to heal, to the praise and glory of your Name; through Jesus Christ our Lord, who lives and reigns with you, in the unity of the Holy Spirit, one God, now and for ever. *Amen.*   [244]

Saint Mark   *April 25*

Almighty God, by the hand of Mark the evangelist you have given to your Church the Gospel of Jesus Christ the Son of God: We thank you for this witness, and pray that we may be firmly grounded in its truth; through Jesus Christ our Lord, who lives and reigns with you and the Holy Spirit, one God, for ever and ever. *Amen.*   [240]

Remembering a martyr

Almighty God, by whose grace and power your holy martyr
N. triumphed over suffering and was faithful even to death:
Grant us, who now remember *him* in thanksgiving, to be so
faithful in our witness to you in this world, that we may
receive with *him* the crown of life; through Jesus Christ our
Lord, who lives and reigns with you and the Holy Spirit, one
God, for ever and ever. *Amen.*   [246]

Saint Mary Magdalene   *July 22*

Almighty God, whose blessed Son restored Mary Magdalene
to health of body and of mind, and called her to be a witness
of his resurrection: Mercifully grant that by your grace we
may be healed from all our infirmities and know you in the
power of his unending life; who with you and the Holy Spirit
lives and reigns, one God, now and for ever. *Amen.*   [242]

Saint Mary the Virgin   *August 15*

O God, you have taken to yourself the blessed Virgin Mary,
mother of your incarnate Son: Grant that we, who have been
redeemed by his blood, may share with her the glory of your
eternal kingdom; through Jesus Christ our Lord, who lives
and reigns with you, in the unity of the Holy Spirit, one God,
now and for ever. *Amen.*   [243]

Saint Matthew   *September 21*

We thank you, heavenly Father, for the witness of your
apostle and evangelist Matthew to the Gospel of your Son
our Savior; and we pray that, after his example, we may with
ready wills and hearts obey the calling of our Lord to follow

him; through Jesus Christ our Lord, who lives and reigns with you and the Holy Spirit, one God, now and for ever. *Amen.* [244]

Saint Matthias *February 24*

Almighty God, who in the place of Judas chose your faithful servant Matthias to be numbered among the Twelve: Grant that your Church, being delivered from false apostles, may always be guided and governed by faithful and true pastors; through Jesus Christ our Lord, who lives and reigns with you, in the unity of the Holy Spirit, one God, now and for ever. *Amen.* [239]

Saint Michael and All Angels *September 29*

Everlasting God, you have ordained and constituted in a wonderful order the ministries of angels and mortals: Mercifully grant that, as your holy angels always serve and worship you in heaven, so by your appointment they may help and defend us here on earth; through Jesus Christ our Lord, who lives and reigns with you and the Holy Spirit, one God, for ever and ever. *Amen.* [244]

Saint Paul *January 25*

O God, by the preaching of your apostle Paul you have caused the light of the Gospel to shine throughout the world: Grant, we pray, that we, having his wonderful conversion in remembrance, may show ourselves thankful to you by following his holy teaching; through Jesus Christ our Lord, who lives and reigns with you, in the unity of the Holy spirit, one God, now and for ever. *Amen.* [238]

Saint Peter   *January* 18

Almighty Father, who inspired Simon Peter, first among the apostles, to confess Jesus as Messiah and Son of the living God: Keep your Church steadfast upon the rock of this faith, so that in unity and peace we may proclaim the one truth and follow the one Lord, our Savior Jesus Christ; who lives and reigns with you and the Holy Spirit, one God, now and for ever. *Amen.*   [238]

Saint Peter and Saint Paul   *June* 29

Almighty God, whose blessed apostles Peter and Paul glorified you by their martyrdom: Grant that your Church, instructed by their teaching and example, and knit together in unity by your Spirit, may ever stand firm upon the one foundation, which is Jesus Christ our Lord; who lives and reigns with you, in the unity of the Holy Spirit, one God, now and for ever. *Amen.*   [241]

Saint Philip and Saint James   *May* 1

Almighty God, who gave to your apostles Philip and James grace and strength to bear witness to the truth: Grant that we, being mindful of their victory of faith, may glorify in life and death the Name of our Lord Jesus Christ; who lives and reigns with you and the Holy Spirit, one God, now and for ever. *Amen.*   [240]

Saint Simon and Saint Jude   *October* 28

O God, we thank you for the glorious company of the apostles, and especially on this day for Simon and Jude; and we pray that, as they were faithful and zealous in their mission, so we may with ardent devotion make known the love and mercy of our Lord and Savior Jesus Christ; who lives and reigns with you and the Holy Spirit, one God, for ever and ever. *Amen.* [245]

Saint Stephen *December 26*

We give you thanks, O Lord of glory, for the example of the first martyr Stephen, who looked up to heaven and prayed for his persecutors to your Son Jesus Christ, who stands at your right hand; where he lives and reigns with you and the Holy Spirit, one God, in glory everlasting. *Amen.* [237]

Saint Thomas *December 21*

Everliving God, who strengthened your apostle Thomas with firm and certain faith in your Son's resurrection: Grant us so perfectly and without doubt to believe in Jesus Christ, our Lord and our God, that our faith may never be found wanting in your sight; through him who lives and reigns with you and the Holy spirit, one God, now and for ever. *Amen.* [237]

Remembering a Saint

Almighty God, you have surrounded us with a great cloud of witnesses: Grant that we, encouraged by the good example of your servant N., may persevere in running the race that is set before us, until at last we may with *him* attain to your eternal joy; through Jesus Christ, the pioneer and perfecter of our faith, who lives and reigns with you and the Holy Spirit, one God, for ever and ever. *Amen.* [250]

For the intercession of the Saints

Almighty and everlasting God, who art the Lord both of the quick and the dead, and hast mercy upon all whom thou foreknowest will be thine in faith and works: we humbly beseech thee that they for whom we have purposed to pour forth our prayers, both those whom this present world still holdeth in the flesh, and those whom the world to come hath already received set free from the body, may at the intercession of all thy Saints, obtain pardon of all their sins by the pitifulness of thy great goodness. Through Jesus Christ thy Son our Lord, who liveth and reigneth with thee, in the unity of the Holy Ghost, ever one God, world without end. *Amen.*   [SAPB, 304]

Defend *us, we* beseech thee, O Lord, from all perils of mind and body: and at the intercession of the blessed and glorious Mary, the Ever-Virgin Mother of God, of blessed Joseph, of thy blessed Apostles Peter and Paul, (and blessed N. *our* patron,) and all Saints, graciously bestow upon *us* both peace and safety: that all adversity and error being done away, thy Church may serve thee in untroubled freedom. Through the same Christ our Lord. *Amen.*   [SAPB, 41]

For faith and love like the Saints

Almighty and everlasting God, who dost enkindle the flame of thy love in the hearts of the Saints; Grant to us, thy humble servants, the same faith and power of love; that, as we rejoice in their triumphs, we may profit by their examples; through Jesus Christ our Lord.
Amen.   [28BCP, 258]

For the support of the Saints

Almighty God, by your Holy Spirit you have made us one
with your saints in heaven and on earth: Grant that in our
earthly pilgrimage we may always be supported by this
fellowship of love and prayer, and know ourselves to be
surrounded by their witness to your power and mercy.
We ask this for the sake of Jesus Christ, in whom all our
intercessions are acceptable through the Spirit, and who lives
and reigns for ever and ever. *Amen.*   [395]

For grace to follow the Saints

Almighty God, you have knit together your elect in one
communion and fellowship in the mystical body of your Son
Christ our Lord: Give us grace so to follow your blessed
saints in all virtuous and godly living, that we may come to
those ineffable joys that you have prepared for those who
truly love you; through Jesus Christ our Lord, who with you
and the Holy Spirit lives and reigns, one God, in glory
everlasting. *Amen.*   [245]

Almighty and everliving God, we yield unto thee most high
praise and hearty thanks, for the wonderful grace and virtue
declared in all thy saints, who have been the choice vessels of
thy grace, and the lights of the world in their several
generations; most humbly beseeching thee to give us grace so
to follow the example of their steadfastness in thy faith, and
obedience to thy holy commandments, that at the day of the
general Resurrection, we, with all those who are of the
mystical body of thy Son, may be set on his right hand, and
hear that his most joyful voice: Come, ye blessed of my
Father, inherit the kingdom prepared for you from the
foundation of the world. Grant this, O Father, for the sake of
the same, thy Son Jesus Christ, our only Mediator and
Advocate. *Amen.*   [28BCP, 336]

The cloud of witnesses

Our heavenly Father, we rejoice in the blessed communion of all thy saints, wherein thou givest us also to have part. We remember before thee all who have departed this life in thy faith and love, and especially those most dear to us. We thank thee for our present fellowship with them, for our common hope, and for the promise of future joy. O, let the cloud of witnesses, the innumerable company of those who have gone before, and entered into rest, be to us an example of godly life, and even now may we be refreshed with their joy; that so with patience we may run the race that yet remains before us, looking unto Jesus, the author and finisher of our faith; and obtain an entrance into the everlasting kingdom, and glorious assembly of the saints, and with them ever worship and adore thy glorious Name, world without end. *Amen.*   [PPB, NO. 593][60]

Advent

Almighty God, give us grace to cast away the works of darkness, and put on the armor of light, now in the time of this mortal life in which your Son Jesus Christ came to visit us in great humility; that in the last day, when he shall come again in his glorious majesty to judge both the living and the dead, we may rise to the life immortal; through him who lives and reigns with you and the Holy Spirit, one God, now and for ever. *Amen.*   [211]

Almighty Father, whose blessed Son at his coming amongst us brought redemption unto his people and peace to men of goodwill: grant that, when he shall come again in glory to judge the world and to make all things new, we may be found ready to receive him, and enter into his joy; through the same our Lord Jesus Christ. *Amen.*   [PPB, NO. 472][16]

Christmas

Almighty and everliving God, you have given us a new revelation of your loving providence in the Coming of your Son Jesus Christ to be born of the Virgin Mary: Grant that as he shared our mortality, so we may share his eternity in the glory of your kingdom; where he lives and reigns for ever and ever. *Amen.*   [BOOS, 34]

O God our Creator, to restore our fallen race you spoke the effectual word, and the Eternal Word became flesh in the womb of the Blessed Virgin Mary: Mercifully grant that as he humbled himself to be clothed with our humanity, so we may be found worthy, in him, to be clothed with his divinity; who lives and reigns for ever and ever. *Amen.*   [BOOS, 35]

Most merciful and loving God, you have made this day holy by the incarnation of your Son Jesus Christ, and by the child-bearing of the Blessed Virgin Mary: Grant that we your people may enter with joy into the celebration of this day, and may also rejoice for ever as your adopted sons and daughters; through Jesus Christ our Lord. *Amen.*   [BOOS, 35]

On New Year's eve

O God our Creator, you have divided our life into days and seasons, and called us to acknowledge your providence year after year: Accept your people who come to offer their praises, and, in your mercy, receive their prayers; through Jesus Christ our Lord. *Amen.*   [BOOS, 40]

Immortal Lord God, you inhabit eternity, and have brought us your unworthy servants to the close of another year: Pardon, we entreat you, our transgressions of the past, and graciously abide with us all the days of our life; through Jesus Christ our Lord. *Amen.*   [BOOS, 42]

Most gracious and merciful God, you have reconciled us to yourself through Jesus Christ your Son, and called us to new life in him: Grant that we, who begin this year in his Name, may complete it to his honor and glory; who lives and reigns now and for ever. *Amen.*   [BOOS, 43]

On Candlemas

God our Father, source of all light, today you revealed to the aged Simeon your light which enlightens the nations. Fill our hearts with the light of faith, that we who bear these candles may walk in the path of goodness, and come to the Light that shines for ever, your Son Jesus Christ our Lord. *Amen.*   [BOOS, 52]

O God, you have made this day holy by the presentation of your Son in the Temple, and by the purification of the Blessed Virgin Mary: Mercifully grant that we, who delight in her humble readiness to be the birth-giver of the Only-begotten, may rejoice for ever in our adoption as his sisters and brothers; through Jesus Christ our Lord. *Amen.*   [BOOS, 53]

Epiphany

We thank thee O God, that thou didst give thy Son Jesus Christ to be the light of the world, and that in him thou hast revealed thy glory and the wonder of thy saving love. Help us to love thee who hast so loved us; strengthen us for the service of thy kingdom; and grant that the light of Christ may so shine throughout the world that men everywhere may be drawn to him who is the Savior and Lord of all, and the whole earth be filled with thy glory, through Jesus Christ, our Lord. *Amen.*   [PPB, NO. 488][61]

O God, who by the leading of a star didst manifest thy
only-begotten Son to the Gentiles; Mercifully grant that we,
who know thee now by faith, may after this life have the
fruition of thy glorious Godhead; through the same thy Son
Jesus Christ our Lord. *Amen.*   [28BCP, 107]

Lent

Grant, most merciful Lord, to your faithful people pardon
and peace, that they may be cleansed from all their sins, and
serve you with a quiet mind; through Christ our Lord.
Amen.   [BOOS, 23]

Grant, Almighty God, that your people may recognize their
weakness and put their whole trust in your strength, so that
they may rejoice for ever in the protection of your loving
providence; through Christ our Lord. *Amen.*   [BOOS, 23]

Keep this your family, Lord, with your never-failing mercy,
that relying solely on the help of your heavenly grace, they
may be upheld by your divine protection; through Christ our
Lord. *Amen.*   [BOOS, 23]

Look mercifully on this your family, Almighty God, that by
your great goodness they may be governed and preserved
evermore; through Christ our Lord. *Amen.*   [BOOS, 23]

Look down in mercy, Lord, on your people who kneel before
you; and grant that those whom you have nourished by your
Word and Sacraments may bring forth fruit worthy of
repentance; through Christ our Lord. *Amen.*   [BOOS, 23]

Look with compassion, O Lord, upon this your people; that,
rightly observing this holy season, they may learn to know
you more fully, and to serve you with a more perfect will;
through Christ our Lord. *Amen.*   [BOOS, 24]

From Palm Sunday through Maundy Thursday

Almighty God, we pray you graciously to behold this your family, for whom our Lord Jesus Christ was willing to be betrayed, and given into the hands of sinners, and to suffer death upon the cross; who lives and reigns for ever and ever. *Amen.* [BOOS, 24]

Palm Sunday

Almighty and everlasting God, who, of thy tender love towards mankind, hast sent thy Son, our Savior Jesus Christ, to take upon him our flesh, and to suffer death upon the cross, that all mankind should follow the example of his great humility; Mercifully grant, that we may both follow the example of his patience, and also be made partakers of his resurrection; through the same Jesus Christ our Lord. *Amen.* [28BCP, 134]

Monday in Holy Week

Almighty God, whose most dear Son went not up to joy but first he suffered pain, and entered not into glory before he was crucified; Mercifully grant that we, walking in the way of the cross, may find it none other than the way of life and peace; through the same thy Son Jesus Christ our Lord. *Amen.* [28BCP, 138]

Tuesday in Holy Week

O Lord God, whose blessed Son, our Savior, gave his back to the smiters and hid not his face from shame; Grant us grace to take joyfully the sufferings of the present time, in full assurance of the glory that shall be revealed; through the same thy Son Jesus Christ our Lord. *Amen.* [28BCP, 144]

Wednesday in Holy Week

Assist us mercifully with thy help, O Lord God of our salvation; that we may enter with joy upon the meditation of those mighty acts, whereby thou hast given unto us life and immortality; through Jesus Christ our Lord. *Amen.*   [28BCP, 147]

Maundy Thursday

Almighty Father, whose dear Son, on the night before he suffered, did institute the Sacrament of his Body and Blood; Mercifully grant that we may thankfully receive the same in remembrance of him, who in these holy mysteries giveth us a pledge of life eternal; the same thy Son Jesus Christ our Lord, who now liveth and reigneth with thee and the Holy Spirit ever, one God, world without end. *Amen.*   [28BCP, 152]

Good Friday

Almighty God, we beseech thee graciously to behold this thy family, for which our Lord Jesus Christ was contented to be betrayed, and given up into the hands of wicked men, and to suffer death upon the cross; who now liveth and reigneth with thee and the Holy Ghost ever, one God, world without end. *Amen.*   [28BCP, 156]

Holy Saturday   *Easter Even*

Grant, O Lord, that as we are baptized into the death of thy blessed Son, our Savior Jesus Christ, so by continual mortifying our corrupt affections we may be buried with him; and that through the grave, and gate of death, we may pass to our joyful resurrection; for his merits, who died, and was buried, and rose again for us, the same thy Son Jesus Christ our Lord. *Amen.*   [28BCP, 161]

O God, who made this most holy night to shine with the glory of the Lord's resurrection: Stir up in your Church that Spirit of adoption which is given to us in Baptism, that we, being renewed both in body and mind, may worship you in sincerity and truth; through Jesus Christ our Lord, who lives and reigns with you, in the unity of the Holy Spirit, one God, now and for ever. *Amen.* [295]

Easter day

Almighty God, who through your only-begotten Son Jesus Christ overcame death and opened to us the gate of everlasting life: Grant that we, who celebrate with joy the day of the Lord's resurrection, may be raised from the death of sin by your life-giving Spirit; through Jesus Christ our Lord, who lives and reigns with you and the Holy Spirit, one God, now and for ever. *Amen.* [222]

O God, who for our redemption didst give thine only-begotten Son to the death of the Cross, and by his glorious resurrection hast delivered us from the power of our enemy; Grant us so to die daily from sin, that we may evermore live with him in the joy of his resurrection; through the same thy Son Christ our Lord. *Amen.* [28BCP, 165]

Ascension day

Grant, we beseech thee, Almighty God, that like as we do believe thy only-begotten Son our Lord Jesus Christ to have ascended into the heavens; so we may also in heart and mind thither ascend, and with him continually dwell, who liveth and reigneth with thee and the Holy Ghost, one God, world without end. *Amen.* [28BCP, 177]

Pentecost

Almighty God, on this day you opened the way of eternal life to every race and nation by the promised gift of your Holy Spirit: Shed abroad this gift throughout the world by the preaching of the Gospel, that it may reach to the ends of the earth; through Jesus Christ our Lord, who lives and reigns with you, in the unity of the Holy Spirit, one God, for ever and ever. *Amen.*   [227]

O God, who on this day taught the hearts of your faithful people by sending to them the light of your Holy Spirit: Grant us by the same Spirit to have a right judgment in all things, and evermore to rejoice in his holy comfort; through Jesus Christ your Son our Lord, who lives, and reigns with you, in the unity of the Holy Spirit, one God, for ever and ever. *Amen.*   [227]

Trinity Sunday

Almighty and everlasting God, who hast given unto us thy servants grace, by the confession of a true faith, to acknowledge the glory of the eternal Trinity, and in the power of the Divine Majesty to worship the Unity; We beseech thee that thou wouldest keep us steadfast in this faith, and evermore defend us from all adversities, who livest and reignest, one God, world without end. *Amen.* [28BCP, 186]

Memorial day

Almighty God, our heavenly Father, in whose hands are the living and the dead; We give thee thanks for all those thy servants who have laid down their lives in the service of our country. Grant to them thy mercy and the light of thy presence, that the good work which thou hast begun in them may be perfected; through Jesus Christ thy Son our Lord. *Amen.* [28BCP, 42]

Independence day

Lord God Almighty, in whose Name the founders of this country won liberty for themselves and for us, and lit the torch of freedom for nations then unborn: Grant that we and all the people of this land may have grace to maintain our liberties in righteousness and peace; through Jesus Christ our Lord, who lives and reigns with you and the Holy Spirit, one God, for ever and ever. *Amen.* [242]

Labor day

Almighty God, you have so linked our lives one with another that all we do affects, for good or ill, all other lives: So guide us in the work we do, that we may do it not for self alone, but for the common good; and, as we seek a proper return for our own labor, make us mindful of the rightful aspirations of other workers, and arouse our concern for those who are out of work; through Jesus Christ our Lord, who lives and reigns with you and the Holy Spirit, one God, for ever and ever. *Amen.* [261]

Thanksgiving day

Almighty and gracious Father, we give you thanks for the fruits of the earth in their season and for the labors of those who harvest them. Make us, we pray, faithful stewards of your great bounty, for the provision of our necessities and the relief of all who are in need, to the glory of your Name; through Jesus Christ our Lord, who lives and reigns with you and the Holy Spirit, one God, now and for ever. *Amen.* [246]

On Sundays

O God our King, by the resurrection of your Son Jesus Christ
on the first day of the week, you conquered sin, put death to
flight, and gave us the hope of everlasting life: Redeem all
our days by this victory; forgive our sins, banish our fears,
make us bold to praise you and to do your will; and steel us
to wait for the consummation of your kingdom on the last
great Day; through the same Jesus Christ our Lord.
Amen. [835]

IX
Litanies

Litanies

The Great Litany

O God the Father, Creator of heaven and earth,
Have mercy upon us.

O God the Son, Redeemer of the world,
Have mercy upon us.

O God the Holy Ghost, Sanctifier of the faithful,
Have mercy upon us.

O holy, blessed, and glorious Trinity, one God,
Have mercy upon us.

Remember not, Lord Christ, our offenses, nor the offenses of
our forefathers; neither reward us according to our sins.
Spare us, good Lord, spare thy people, whom thou hast
redeemed with thy most precious blood, and by thy mercy
preserve us for ever.
Spare us, good Lord.

From all evil and wickedness; from sin; from the crafts and
assaults of the devil; and from everlasting damnation,
Good Lord, deliver us.

From all blindness of heart; from pride, vainglory, and
hypocrisy; from envy, hatred, and malice; and from all want
of charity,
Good Lord, deliver us.

From all inordinate and sinful affections; and from all the
deceits of the world, the flesh, and the devil,
Good Lord, deliver us.

From all false doctrine, heresy, and schism; from hardness of heart, and contempt of thy Word and commandment,
Good Lord, deliver us.

From lightning and tempest; from earthquake, fire, and flood; from plague, pestilence, and famine,
Good Lord, deliver us.

From all oppression, conspiracy, and rebellion; from violence, battle, and murder; and from dying suddenly and unprepared,
Good Lord, deliver us.

By the mystery of thy holy Incarnation; by thy holy Nativity and submission to the Law; by thy Baptism, Fasting, and Temptation,
Good Lord, deliver us.

By thine Agony and Bloody Sweat; by thy Cross and Passion; by thy precious Death and Burial; by thy glorious Resurrection and Ascension; and by the Coming of the Holy Ghost,
Good Lord, deliver us.

In all time of our tribulation; in all time of our prosperity; in the hour of death, and in the day of judgment,
Good Lord, deliver us.

We sinners do beseech thee to hear us, O Lord God; and that it may please thee to rule and govern thy holy Church Universal in the right way,
We beseech thee to hear us, good Lord.

That it may please thee to illumine all bishops, priests, and deacons, with true knowledge and understanding of thy Word; and that both by their preaching and living, they may set it forth, and show it accordingly,
We beseech thee to hear us, good Lord.

That it may please thee to bless and keep all thy people,
We beseech thee to hear us, good Lord.

That it may please thee to send forth laborers into thy harvest, and to draw all mankind into thy kingdom,
We beseech thee to hear us, good Lord.

That it may please thee to give to all people increase of grace to hear and receive thy Word, and to bring forth the fruits of the Spirit,
We beseech thee to hear us, good Lord.

That it may please thee to bring into the way of truth all such as have erred, and are deceived,
We beseech thee to hear us, good Lord.

That it may please thee to give us a heart to love and fear thee, and diligently to live after thy commandments,
We beseech thee to hear us, good Lord.

That it may please thee so to rule the hearts of thy servants, the President of the United States (*or* of this nation), and all others in authority, that they may do justice, and love mercy, and walk in the ways of truth,
We beseech thee to hear us, good Lord.

That it may please thee to make wars to cease in all the world; to give to all nations unity, peace, and concord; and to bestow freedom upon all peoples,
We beseech thee to hear us, good Lord.

That it may please thee to show thy pity upon all prisoners and captives, the homeless and the hungry, and all who are desolate and oppressed,
We beseech thee to hear us, good Lord.

That it may please thee to give and preserve to our use the bountiful fruits of the earth, so that in due time all may enjoy them,
We beseech thee to hear us, good Lord.

That it may please thee to inspire us, in our several callings, to do the work which thou givest us to do with singleness of heart as thy servants, and for the common good,
We beseech thee to hear us, good Lord.

That it may please thee to preserve all who are in danger by reason of their labor or their travel,
We beseech thee to hear us, good Lord.

That it may please thee to preserve, and provide for, all women in childbirth, young children and orphans, the widowed, and all whose homes are broken or torn by strife,
We beseech thee to hear us, good Lord.

That it may please thee to visit the lonely; to strengthen all who suffer in mind, body, and spirit; and to comfort with thy presence those who are failing and infirm,
We beseech thee to hear us, good Lord.

That it may please thee to support, help, and comfort all who are in danger, necessity, and tribulation,
We beseech thee to hear us, good Lord.

That it may please thee to have mercy upon all mankind,
We beseech thee to hear us, good Lord.

That it may please thee to give us true repentance; to forgive us all our sins, negligences, and ignorances; and to endue us with the grace of thy Holy Spirit to amend our lives according to thy holy Word,
We beseech thee to hear us, good Lord.

That it may please thee to forgive our enemies, persecutors, and slanderers, and to turn their hearts,
We beseech thee to hear us, good Lord.

That it may please thee to strengthen such as do stand; to comfort and help the weak-hearted; to raise up those who fall; and finally to beat down Satan under our feet,
We beseech thee to hear us, good Lord.

That it may please thee to grant to all the faithful departed eternal life and peace,
We beseech thee to hear us, good Lord.

That it may please thee to grant that, in the fellowship of
(_____ and) all the saints, we may attain to thy heavenly
kingdom,
We beseech thee to hear us, good Lord.

Son of God, we beseech thee to hear us.
Son of God, we beseech thee to hear us.

O Lamb of God, that takest away the sins of the world,
Have mercy upon us.

O Lamb of God, that takest away the sins of the world,
Have mercy upon us.

O Lamb of God, that takest away the sins of the world,
Grant us thy peace.

O Christ, hear us.
O Christ, hear us.

Lord, have mercy upon us.		Kyrie eleison.
Christ, have mercy upon us.	*or*	*Christe eleison.*
Lord, have mercy upon us.		Kyrie eleison.

*When the Litany is sung or said immediately before the Eucharist, the
Litany concludes here, and the Eucharist begins with the Salutation and
the Collect of the Day.*

On all other occasions, the Officiant and People say together

Our Father, who art in heaven,
    hallowed be thy name,
    thy kingdom come,
    thy will be done,
        on earth as it is in heaven.
Give us this day our daily bread.
And forgive us our trespasses,
    as we forgive those who trespass against us.
And lead us not into temptation,
    but deliver us from evil. *Amen.*

V.   O Lord, let thy mercy be showed upon us;
R.   As we do put our trust in thee.

The Officiant concludes with the following or some other Collect

Let us pray.

Almighty God, who hast promised to hear the petitions of those who ask in thy Son's Name: We beseech thee mercifully to incline thine ear to us who have now made our prayers and supplications unto thee; and grant that those things which we have asked faithfully according to thy will, may be obtained effectually, to the relief of our necessity, and to the setting forth of thy glory; through Jesus Christ our Lord. *Amen.* [148]

Litany for the departed

For our brother (sister) N., let us pray to our Lord Jesus Christ who said, "I am Resurrection and I am Life."

Lord, you consoled Martha and Mary in their distress; draw near to us who mourn for N., and dry the tears of those who weep.
Hear us, Lord.

You wept at the grave of Lazarus, your friend; comfort us in our sorrow.
Hear us, Lord.

You raised the dead to life; give to our brother (sister) eternal life.
Hear us, Lord.

You promised paradise to the thief who repented; bring our brother (sister) to the joys of heaven.
Hear us, Lord.

Our brother (sister) was washed in Baptism and anointed with the Holy Spirit; give *him* fellowship with all your saints.
Hear us, Lord.

He was nourished with your Body and Blood; grant *him* a place at the table in your heavenly kingdom.
Hear us, Lord.

Comfort us in our sorrows at the death of our brother (sister); let our faith be our consolation, and eternal life our hope.

Silence may be kept.

The Celebrant concludes with one of the following or some other prayer

Lord Jesus Christ, we commend to you our brother (sister) N., who was reborn by water and the Spirit in Holy Baptism. Grant that *his* death may recall to us your victory over death, and be an occasion for us to renew our trust in your Father's love. Give us, we pray, the faith to follow where you have led the way; and where you live and reign with the Father and the Holy Spirit, to the ages of ages. *Amen.*

or this

Father of all, we pray to you for N., and for all those whom we love but see no longer. Grant to them eternal rest. Let light perpetual shine upon them. May *his* soul and the souls of all the departed, through the mercy of God, rest in peace. *Amen.* [497]

Litany at the time of death

God the Father,
Have mercy on your servant.

God the Son,
Have mercy on your servant.

God the Holy Spirit,
Have mercy on your servant.

Holy Trinity, one God,
Have mercy on your servant.

From all evil, from all sin, from all tribulation,
Good Lord, deliver him.

By your holy Incarnation, by your Cross and Passion, by
your precious Death and Burial,
Good Lord, deliver him.

By your glorious Resurrection and Ascension, and by the
Coming of the Holy Spirit,
Good Lord, deliver him.

We sinners beseech you to hear us, Lord Christ: That it may
please you to deliver the soul of your servant from the power
of evil, and from eternal death,
We beseech you to hear us, good Lord.

That it may please you mercifully to pardon all *his* sins.
We beseech you to hear us, good Lord.

That it may please you to grant *him* a place of refreshment
and everlasting blessedness,
We beseech you to hear us, good Lord.

That it may please you to give *him* joy and gladness in your
kingdom, with your saints in light,
We beseech you to hear us, good Lord.

Jesus, Lamb of God:
Have mercy on him.

Jesus, bearer of our sins:
Have mercy on him.

Jesus, redeemer of the world:
Give him *your peace.*

Lord, have mercy.
Christ, have mercy.
Lord, have mercy.

Our Father, who art in heaven
  hallowed be thy name.
  thy kingdom come,
  thy will be done,
  on earth as it is in heaven.
Give us this day our daily bread.
And forgive us our trespasses,
  as we forgive those who trespass against us.
And lead us not into temptation,
  but deliver us from evil. *Amen.*

The Officiant says this Collect

Let us pray.

Deliver your servant, N., O Sovereign Lord Christ, from all evil, and set *him* free from every bond; that *he* may rest with all your saints in the eternal habitations; where with the Father and the Holy Spirit you live and reign, one God, for ever and ever. *Amen.*   [462]

Litany of Thanksgiving for the nation

Almighty God, giver of all good things: We thank you for the natural majesty and beauty of this land. They restore us, though we often destroy them.
Heal us.

We thank you for the great resources of this nation. They make us rich, though we often exploit them.
Forgive us.

We thank you for the men and women who have made this country strong. They are models for us, though we often fall short of them.
Inspire us.

We thank you for the torch of liberty which has been lit in this land. It has drawn people from every nation, though we have often hidden from its light.
Enlighten us.

We thank you for the faith we have inherited in all its rich variety. It sustains our life, though we have been faithless again and again.
Renew us.

Help us, O Lord, to finish the good work here begun. Strengthen our efforts to blot out ignorance and prejudice, and to abolish poverty and crime. And hasten the day when all our people, with many voices in one united chorus, will glorify your holy Name. *Amen.*   [838]

Litany of Thanksgiving for a church

Let us thank God whom we worship here in the beauty of holiness.

Eternal God, the heaven of heavens cannot contain you, much less the walls of temples made with hands. Graciously receive our thanks for this place, and accept the work of our hands, offered to your honor and glory.

For the Church universal, of which these visible buildings are the symbol,
We thank you, Lord.

For your presence whenever two or three have gathered together in your Name,
We thank you, Lord.

For this place where we may be still and know that you are God,
We thank you, Lord.

For making us your children by adoption and grace, and refreshing us day by day with the bread of life.
We thank you, Lord.

For the knowledge of your will and the grace to perform it,
We thank you, Lord.

For the fulfilling of our desires and petitions as you see best
for us,
We thank you, Lord.

For the pardon of our sins, which restores us to the company
of your faithful people,
We thank you, Lord.

For the blessing of our vows and the crowning of our years
with your goodness,
We thank you, Lord.

For the faith of those who have gone before us and for our
encouragement by their perseverance,
We thank you, Lord.

For the fellowship of (*N.*, our patron, and of) all your Saints,
We thank you, Lord.

After a brief silence, the Celebrant concludes with the following Doxology

Yours, O Lord, is the greatness, the power, the
glory, the victory, and the majesty;
People   For everything in heaven and on earth is yours.
Celebrant   Yours, O Lord, is the kingdom;
People   And you are exalted as head over all. *Amen.*   [578]

A Litany of healing

The Celebrant introduces the Litany with this bidding

Let us name before God those for whom we offer our
prayers.

The People audibly name those for whom they are interceding.

A Person appointed then leads the Litany

God the Father, your will for all people is health and
salvation;
We praise you and thank you, O Lord.

God the Son, you came that we might have life, and might
have it more abundantly;
We praise you and thank you, O Lord.

God the Holy Spirit, you make our bodies the temple of your
presence;
We praise you and thank you, O Lord.

Holy Trinity, one God, in you we live and move and have our
being;
We praise you and thank you, O Lord.

Lord, grant your healing grace to all who are sick, injured, or
disabled, that they may be made whole;
Hear us, O Lord of life.

Grant to all who seek your guidance, and to all who are
lonely, anxious, or despondent, a knowledge of your will and
an awareness of your presence;
Hear us, O Lord of life.

Mend broken relationships, and restore those in emotional
distress to soundness of mind and serenity of spirit;
Hear us, O Lord of life.

Bless physicians, nurses, and all others who minister to the
suffering, granting them wisdom and skill, sympathy and
patience;
Hear us, O Lord of life.

Grant to the dying peace and a holy death, and uphold by the
grace and consolation of your Holy Spirit those who are
bereaved;
Hear us, O Lord of life.

Restore to wholeness whatever is broken by human sin, in
our lives, in our nation, and in the world;
Hear us, O Lord of life.

You are the Lord who does wonders:
You have declared your power among the peoples.

With you, O Lord, is the well of life:
And in your light we see light.

Hear us, O Lord of life:
Heal us, and make us whole.

Let us pray.

A period of silence follows.

The Celebrant concludes the Prayers with one of the following or some other suitable Collect:

Almighty God, giver of life and health: Send your blessing on all who are sick, and upon those who minister to them, that all weakness may be vanquished by the triumph of the risen Christ; who lives and reigns for ever and ever. *Amen.*

or this

Heavenly Father, you have promised to hear what we ask in the Name of your Son: Accept and fulfill our petitions, we pray, not as we ask in our ignorance, nor as we deserve in our sinfulness, but as you know and love us in your Son Jesus Christ our Lord. *Amen.*

or this

O Lord our God, accept the fervent prayers of your people; in the multitude of your mercies look with compassion upon us and all who turn to you for help; for you are gracious, O lover of souls, and to you we give glory, Father, Son, and Holy Spirit, now and for ever. *Amen.*   [BOOS, 148]

A Litany for Ordinations

For use at Ordinations as directed. On Ember Days or other occasions, if desired, this Litany may be used for the Prayers of the People at the Eucharist or the Daily Office, or it may be used separately.

God the Father,
Have mercy on us.

God the Son,
Have mercy on us.

God the Holy Spirit,
Have mercy on us.

Holy Trinity, one God,
Have mercy on us.

We pray to you, Lord Christ.
Lord, hear our prayer.

For the holy Church of God, that it may be filled with truth and love, and be found without fault at the Day of your Coming,
we pray to you, O Lord.
Lord, hear our prayer.

For all members of your Church in their vocation and ministry, that they may serve you in a true and godly life,
we pray to you, O Lord.
Lord, hear our prayer.

For N., our Presiding Bishop, and for all bishops, priests, and deacons, that they may be filled with your love, may hunger for truth, and may thirst after righteousness,
we pray to you, O Lord.
Lord, hear our prayer.

For N., chosen bishop (priest, deacon) in your Church,
we pray to you, O Lord.
Lord, hear our prayer.

That *he* may faithfully fulfill the duties of this ministry, build up your Church, and glorify your Name,
we pray to you, O Lord.
Lord, hear our prayer.

That by the indwelling of the Holy Spirit *he* may be sustained and encouraged to persevere to the end,
we pray to you, O Lord.
Lord, hear our prayer.

For *his* family [the members of *his* household *or* community], that they may be adorned with all Christian virtues,
we pray to you, O Lord.
Lord, hear our prayer.

For all who fear God and believe in you, Lord Christ, that our divisions may cease and that all may be one as you and the Father are one,
we pray to you, O Lord.
Lord, hear our prayer.

For the mission of the Church, that in faithful witness it may preach the Gospel to the ends of the earth,
we pray to you, O Lord.
Lord, hear our prayer.

For those who do not yet believe, and for those who have lost their faith, that they may receive the light of the Gospel,
we pray to you, O Lord.
Lord, hear our prayer.

For the peace of the world, that a spirit of respect and forbearance may grow among nations and peoples,
we pray to you, O Lord.
Lord, hear our prayer.

For those in positions of public trust [especially _____], that they may serve justice and promote the dignity and freedom of every person,
we pray to you, O Lord.
Lord, hear our prayer.

For a blessing upon all human labor, and for the right use of the riches of creation, that the world may be freed from poverty, famine, and disaster,
we pray to you, O Lord.
Lord, hear our prayer.

For the poor, the persecuted, the sick, and all who suffer; for refugees, prisoners, and all who are in danger; that they may be relieved and protected,
we pray to you, O Lord.
Lord, hear our prayer.

For ourselves; for the forgiveness of our sins, and for the grace of the Holy Spirit to amend our lives,
we pray to you, O Lord.
Lord, hear our prayer.

For all who have died in the communion of your Church, and those whose faith is known to you alone, that, with all the saints, they may have rest in that place where there is no pain or grief, but life eternal,
we pray to you, O Lord.
Lord, hear our prayer.

Rejoicing in the fellowship of [the ever-blessed Virgin Mary, (*blessed N.*) and] all the saints, let us commend ourselves, and one another, and all our life to Christ our God.
To you, O Lord our God.

Lord, have mercy.
Christ, have mercy.
Lord, have mercy.

At ordinations, the Bishop who is presiding stands and says

The Lord be with you.
People And also with you.
Bishop Let us pray.

The Bishop says the appointed Collect.

When this Litany is used on other occasions, the Officiant concludes with a suitable Collect. [548]

254

A Litany of Thanksgiving

Let us give thanks to God our Father for all his gifts so freely
bestowed upon us.

For the beauty and wonder of your creation, in earth and sky
and sea,
We thank you, Lord.

For all that is gracious in the lives of men and women,
revealing the image of Christ,
We thank you, Lord.

For our daily food and drink, our homes and families, and
our friends,
We thank you, Lord.

For minds to think, and hearts to love, and hands to serve,
We thank you, Lord.

For health and strength to work, and leisure to rest and play,
We thank you, Lord.

For the brave and courageous, who are patient in suffering
and faithful in adversity,
We thank you, Lord.

For all valiant seekers after truth, liberty, and justice,
We thank you, Lord.

For the communion of saints, in all times and places,
We thank you, Lord.

Above all, we give you thanks for the great mercies and
promises given to us in Christ Jesus our Lord;
*To him be praise and glory, with you, O Father, and the Holy
Spirit, now and for ever. Amen.*

[837]

Litany for a church ground breaking

God the Father, Creator of heaven and earth,
Have mercy on us.

God the Son, Redeemer of the world,
Have mercy on us.

God the Holy Spirit, Sanctifier of the faithful,
Have mercy on us.

Holy, blessed, and glorious Trinity, one God,
Have mercy on us.

O Christ the Rock, on which your people, as living stones
joined together, grow into a spiritual house;
Defend your Church, we pray.

O Christ the Vine, of which your people are the branches;
Defend your Church, we pray.

O Christ the Head of the Body, of which your people are the
members;
Defend your Church, we pray.

O Christ our Prophet, you teach the way of God in truth;
Defend your Church, we pray.

O Christ our Priest, you offered yourself upon the Cross, and
now make intercession for us to the Father;
Defend your Church, we pray.

O Christ our King, you reign over all the earth, and make us
citizens of your heavenly kingdom;
Defend your Church, we pray.

O Christ, you sent the Holy Spirit upon the Church, clothing
it with power from on high;
Defend your Church, we pray.

We pray to you, Lord Christ.
Lord, hear our prayer.

That we may be devoted to the Apostles' teaching and
fellowship, to the breaking of bread and the prayers,
Lord, hear our prayer.

That we may make disciples of all nations, baptizing them in
the Name of the Father, and of the Son, and of the Holy
Spirit,
Lord, hear our prayer.

That you will fulfill your promise to be with us always, even
to the ages of ages,
Lord, hear our prayer.

That you will sustain all members of your holy Church, that
in our vocation and ministry we may truly and devoutly
serve you,
Lord, hear our prayer.

That you will bless the clergy of your Church, that they may
diligently preach the Gospel and faithfully celebrate the holy
Sacraments,
Lord, hear our prayer.

That you will heal the divisions in your Church, that all may
be one, even as you and the Father are one,
Lord, hear our prayer.

Arise, O God, maintain your cause;
Do not forget the lives of the poor.

Look down from heaven, behold and tend this vine;
Preserve what your right hand has planted.

Let your priests be clothed with righteousness;
Let your faithful people sing with joy.

The Celebrant says

       The Lord be with you.
People   And also with you.
Celebrant Let us pray.

Let your continual mercy cleanse and defend your Church, O Lord; and, because it cannot continue in safety without your help, protect and govern it always by your goodness; through Jesus Christ our Lord, who lives and reigns with you and the Holy Spirit, one God, for ever and ever. *Amen.*

Glory to God whose power, working in us, can do infinitely more than we ask or imagine: Glory to him from generation to generation in the Church, and in Christ Jesus for ever and ever. *Amen.*   [BOOS, 195]

A Litany for catechumens

In peace let us pray to the Lord, saying "Lord, have mercy."

For *these catechumens*, that *they* may remember this day on which *they were* chosen, and remain for ever grateful for this heavenly blessing, let us pray to the Lord.
Lord, have mercy.

That *they* may use this Lenten season wisely, joining with us in acts of self-denial and in performing works of mercy, let us pray to the Lord.
Lord, have mercy.

For *their* teachers, that they may make known to those whom they teach the riches of the Word of God, let us pray to the Lord.
Lord, have mercy.

For *their* sponsor(s), that in *their* private *lives* and public actions *they* may show to *these candidates* a pattern of life in accordance with the Gospel, let us pray to the Lord.
Lord, have mercy.

For *their families* and friends, that they may place no obstacles in the way of *these candidates*, but rather assist *them* to follow the promptings of the Spirit, let us pray to the Lord.
Lord, have mercy.

For this congregation, that [during this Lenten season] it may abound in love and persevere in prayer, let us pray to the Lord.
Lord, have mercy.

For our Bishop, and for all the clergy and people, let us pray to the Lord.
Lord, have mercy.

For our President, for the leaders of the nations, and for all in authority, let us pray to the Lord.
Lord, have mercy.

For the sick and the sorrowful, and for those in any need or trouble, let us pray to the Lord.
Lord, have mercy.

For _____ , let us pray to the Lord.
Lord, have mercy.

For all who have died in the hope of the resurrection, and for all the departed, let us pray to the Lord.
Lord, have mercy.

In the communion of [_____ and of all the] saints, let us commend ourselves, and one another, and all our life, to Christ our God.
To you, O Lord our God.

Silence

The Celebrant says the following prayer with hands extended over the candidates

Immortal God, Lord Jesus Christ, the protector of all who come to you, the life of those who believe, and the resurrection of the dead: We call upon you for *these* your *servants* who *desire* the grace of spiritual rebirth in the Sacrament of Holy Baptism. Accept *them*, Lord Christ, as you promised when you said, "Ask, and it will be given you; seek, and you will find; knock, and it will be opened to you." Give now, we pray, to those who ask, let those who seek find, open the gate to those who knock; that *these* your *servants* may receive the everlasting benediction of your heavenly washing, and come to that promised kingdom which you have prepared, and where you live and reign for ever and ever. *Amen.*   [BOOS, 122]

Morning Litany

O God, the Father of Heaven,
  O God, the Son, Redeemer of the world,
    O God, the Holy Ghost, Sanctifier of thy people;
Hear us, we beseech thee, O Lord.

We, in communion with all thy saints in all ages, with patriarchs and prophets, with apostles and martyrs, with all who have passed from us into thy presence, we, who are still striving to do and to bear thy blessed will on earth, Adore thee, and offer to thee our praises, thanksgivings and supplications.
Hear us, we beseech thee, O Lord.

We pray thee to reveal to us
  the gladness of thy service,
    the beauty of thy perfect will,
      the power of thy presence in our hearts.
Hear us, we beseech thee, O Lord.

Help us to forgive as we would be forgiven, dwelling neither in speech nor thought upon offences committed against us, but loving one another as thou lovest us.
Hear us, we beseech thee, O Lord.

Make us of quick and tender conscience, that we may follow every suggestion of thine indwelling Spirit.
Hear us, we beseech thee, O Lord.

Amen.   [PPB, NO. 6]⁶⁴

A Litany for personal life

The Southwell Litany, originally composed and particularly suitable for retreats and quiet days.

Lord, open our minds to see ourselves as you see us,
   or even as others see us and we see others;
And from all unwillingness to know our infirmities,
Save us and help us, O Lord.

From moral weakness, from hesitation,
   from fear of men and dread of responsibility:
Strengthen us with courage to speak the truth
      in love and self-control;
And alike from the weakness of hasty violence
      and from the weakness of moral cowardice,
Save us and help us, O Lord.

From weakness of judgment,
   from the indecision
      that can make no choice, and
   from the irresolution
      that carries no choice into act:
Strengthen our eye to see and
      our will to choose the right;
And from losing opportunities to serve you,
      and from perplexing ourselves and others with uncertainties,
Save us and help us, O Lord.

From infirmity of purpose
   from want of earnest care and interest,
from sluggish indolence and slack indifference,
      and from all spiritual deadness of heart,
Save us and help us, O Lord.

From dullness of conscience, from feeble sense of duty,
   from thoughtless disregard of consequences to others,
from a low idea of the obligations of our calling,
      and from all half-heartedness in our service,
Save us and help us, O Lord.

From weariness in continuing struggles,
    from despondency in failure and disappointment,
from overburdened sense of unworthiness,
    from morbid fancies of imaginary back-slidings:
Raise us to a lively hope in your mercy
        and in the power of faith;
And from all exaggerated fears and vexations,
Save us and help us, O Lord.

From self-conceit, vanity, and boasting,
    from delight in supposed success and superiority:
Raise us to the modesty and humility
        of true sense and taste and reality;
And from all the harms and hindrances
        of offensive manners and self-assertion,
Save us and help us, O Lord.

From affectation and untruth, conscious or unconscious,
    from pretence and hypocrisy,
from impulsive self-adaptation to the moment
    to please persons or make circumstances easy:
Strengthen us to true simplicity;
        and from all false appearances,
Save us and help us, O Lord.

From love of flattery, from over-ready belief in praise,
    from dislike of criticism,
and from the comfort of self-deception in persuading ourselves
        that others think better of us than we are,
Save us and help us, O Lord.

From all love of display and sacrifice to popularity,
    from thinking of ourselves and forgetting you in our worship:
Hold our minds in spiritual reverence;
        And from self-glorification in all our words and works,
Save us and help us, O Lord.

From pride and self-will,
    from the desire to have our own way in all things,
from overweening love of our own ideas
    and blindness to the value of others,
from resentment against opposition
    and contempt for the claims of others:
Enlarge the generosity of our hearts
    and enlighten the fairness of our judgments;
And from all selfish arbitrariness of temper,
Save us and help us, O Lord.

From jealousy, whether of equals or superiors,
    from grudging others success,
from impatience of submission
    and eagerness for authority:
Give us the spirit of brotherhood
    to share loyally with fellow-workers in all true proportion;
And from all insubordination to just law and proper authority,
Save us and help us, O Lord.

From all hasty utterances of impatience,
    from the retort of irritation and the taunt of sarcasm,
from all infirmity of temper in provoking or being provoked;
    and from all idle words that may do hurt,
Save us and help us, O Lord.

In all times of temptation to follow pleasure,
    to leave duty for amusement,
to indulge in distraction, dissipation, dishonesty, or debt,
    or to degrade our high calling and forget our solemn vows;
And in all times of frailty in our flesh,
Save us and help us, O Lord.

In all times of ignorance and perplexity
    as to what is right and best to do:
Direct us with wisdom to judge aright, and order our ways,
    and overrule our circumstances by your good Providence;
And in our mistakes and misunderstandings,
Save us and help us, O Lord.

In times of doubts and questionings,
    when our belief is perplexed by new learning,
and our faith is strained
    by doctrines and mysteries beyond our understanding:
Give us the faithfulness of learners,
    and the courage of believers in your truth;
And alike from stubborn rejection of new revelations
    and from hasty assurance that we are wiser than our fathers,
Save us and help us, O Lord.

From strife, partisanship, and division,
    from magnifying our certainties to condemn all differences,
from building our systems to exclude all challenges,
    and from all arrogance in our dealings with other persons,
Save us and help us, O Lord.

Give us knowledge of ourselves:
    our power and weaknesses, our spirit, our sympathy,
    our imagination, our knowledge, our truth;
Teach us by the standard of your Word,
    by the judgments of others,
    by examinations of ourselves;
Give us an earnest desire to strengthen ourselves continually
    by study, by diligence, by prayer and meditation;
And from all fancies, delusions,
    and prejudices of habit, or temper, or society,
Save us and help us, O Lord.

Give us true knowledge of others,
   in their difference from us
     and in their likeness to us,
that we may deal with their real selves — measuring
   their feelings by our own, but patiently considering
     their varied lives and thoughts and circumstances;
And in all our dealings with them,
   from false judgments of our own,
     from misplaced trust and distrust,
   from misplaced giving and refusing,
     from misplaced praise and rebuke,
Save us and help us, O Lord.

Chiefly we pray that we may know you
   and see you in all your works,
always feel your presence near,
   hear you and know your call:
Let your Spirit be our will,
     your Word our word;
And in all our shortcomings and infirmities,
   may we have sure faith in your mercy.
Save us and help us, O Lord.

Finally, we pray, blot out our past transgressions,
   heal the evils of our past negligences and ignorances,
and help us to amend
   our past mistakes and misunderstandings:
Uplift our hearts to new love, new energy, new devotion,
   that we may be unburdened from the grief and shame
     of past unfaithfulness,
and go forth in your strength to persevere
   through success and failure,
     through good report and evil report, even to the end;
And in all time of our tribulation,
   and in all time of our prosperity,
Save us and help us, O Lord.

[PTL, 98][62]

A Litany for the mission of the Church

O Father, Creator, from whom the whole family in heaven
and earth is named,
Have mercy on us.

O Son, Redeemer, through whom the world is reconciled to
the Father,
Have mercy on us.

O Holy Spirit, Sanctifier, whose glory fills the world and
searches the deep things of God,
Have mercy on us.

O Holy, blessed, and glorious Trinity, one God,
Have mercy on us.

From blind hearts and petty spirits, that refuse to see the
need of all mankind for your love,
Good Lord, deliver us.

From pride, self-sufficiency, and the unwillingness to admit
our need of your compassion,
Good Lord, deliver us.

From discouragement in the face of pain and disappointment,
and from lack of persistence and thoroughness,
Good Lord, deliver us.

By your baptism into the sins of the world,
Good Lord, forgive us.

By your abundant feeding of the multitudes,
Good Lord, nourish us.

By your suffering and death, which broke down the dividing
walls of hostility among men,
Good Lord, reconcile us.

By your glorious resurrection and ascension,
Good Lord, renew us.

By your commission to the Apostles,
Good Lord, send us forth.

By the coming of the Holy Spirit, who unites all things in heaven and earth,
Good Lord, make us one.

Strengthen and encourage all who do your work in lonely and dangerous places.
Hear us, good Lord.

Open the hearts and hands of many for the support of your Church in every place.
Hear us, good Lord.

Touch our eyes, that we may see the glory of God in all creation.
Hear us, good Lord.

Touch our ears, that we may hear from every mouth the wonderful works of God.
Hear us, good Lord.

Touch our lips, that we may tell in every tongue the wonderful works of God.
Hear us, good Lord.

Touch our hands, that we may do the truth which you have taught us.
Hear us, good Lord.

Touch our feet, that we may go for you into all parts of the world.
Hear us, good Lord.

If the Lord's Prayer is not used elsewhere in the service, it follows here. This collect may be added:

The Collect

O God, without whom our labor is in vain, and with whom the least of your children go forth as the mighty: Prosper all work undertaken according to your will; and grant to all whom you send a pure intention, patient faith, sufficient success upon earth, and the blessedness of serving you in heaven; through Jesus Christ our Lord. *Amen.* [PTL, 93][63]

Litany for sound government

O Lord our Governor, bless the leaders of our land, that we may be a people at peace among ourselves and a blessing to other nations of the earth.
Lord, keep this nation under your care.

To the President and members of the Cabinet, to Governors of States, Mayors of Cities, and to all in administrative authority, grant wisdom and grace in the exercise of their duties.
Give grace to your servants, O Lord.

To Senators and Representatives, and those who make our laws in States, Cities, and Towns, give courage, wisdom, and foresight to provide for the needs of all our people, and to fulfill our obligations in the community of nations.
Give grace to your servants, O Lord.

To the Judges and officers of our Courts give understanding and integrity, that human rights may be safeguarded and justice served.
Give grace to your servants, O Lord.

And finally, teach our people to rely on your strength and to accept their responsibilities to their fellow citizens, that they may elect trustworthy leaders and make wise decisions for the well-being of our society; that we may serve you faithfully in our generation and honor your holy Name.
For yours is the kingdom, O Lord, and you are exalted as head above all. Amen.

[821]

X
General Intercessions and Bidding Prayers

for congregational worship

General Intercessions and Bidding Prayers

for congregational worship

Form 1

Deacon or other leader

With all our heart and with all our mind, let us pray to the Lord, saying, "Lord, have mercy."

For the peace from above, for the loving kindness of God, and for the salvation of our souls, let us pray to the Lord.
Lord, have mercy.

For the peace of the world, for the welfare of the holy Church of God, and for the unity of all peoples, let us pray to the Lord.
Lord, have mercy.

For our Bishop, and for all the clergy and people, let us pray to the Lord.
Lord, have mercy.

For our President, for the leaders of the nations, and for all in authority, let us pray to the Lord.
Lord, have mercy.

For this city (town, village, _____), for every city and community, and for those who live in them, let us pray to the Lord.
Lord, have mercy.

For seasonable weather, and for an abundance of the fruits of the earth, let us pray to the Lord.
Lord, have mercy.

For the good earth which God has given us, and for the
wisdom and will to conserve it, let us pray to the Lord.
Lord, have mercy.

For those who travel on land, on water, or in the air [or
through outer space], let us pray to the Lord.
Lord, have mercy.

For the aged and infirm, for the widowed and orphans, and
for the sick and the suffering, let us pray to the Lord.
Lord, have mercy.

For _____ , let us pray to the Lord.
Lord, have mercy.

For the poor and the oppressed, for the unemployed and
the destitute, for prisoners and captives, and for all who
remember and care for them, let us pray to the Lord.
Lord, have mercy.

For all who have died in the hope of the resurrection, and for
all the departed, let us pray to the Lord.
Lord, have mercy.

For deliverance from all danger, violence, oppression, and
degradation, let us pray to the Lord.
Lord, have mercy.

For the absolution and remission of our sins and offenses, let
us pray to the Lord.
Lord, have mercy.

That we may end our lives in faith and hope, without
suffering and without reproach, let us pray to the Lord.
Lord, have mercy.

Defend us, deliver us, and in thy compassion protect us,
O Lord, by thy grace.
Lord, have mercy.

In the communion of (_____ and of all the) saints, let us
commend ourselves, and one another, and all our life, to
Christ our God.
To thee, O Lord our God.

Silence

The Celebrant adds a concluding Collect.

[383]

Form 11

*In the course of the silence after each bidding, the People offer their own
prayers, either silently or aloud.*

I ask your prayers for God's people throughout the world;
for our Bishop(s) _____ ; for this gathering; and for all
ministers and people.
Pray for the Church.

Silence

I ask your prayers for peace; for goodwill among nations;
and for the well-being of all people.
Pray for justice and peace.

Silence

I ask your prayers for the poor, the sick, the hungry, the
oppressed, and those in prison.
Pray for those in any need or trouble.

Silence

I ask your prayers for all who seek God, or a deeper
knowledge of him.
Pray that they may find and be found by him.

Silence

I ask your prayers for the departed (especially _____).
Pray for those who have died.

Silence

Members of the congregation may ask the prayers or the thanksgivings of those present

I ask your prayers for _____ .

I ask your thanksgiving for _____ .

Silence

Praise God for those in every generation in whom Christ has been honored (especially _____ whom we remember today). Pray that we may have grace to glorify Christ in our own day.

Silence

The Celebrant adds a concluding Collect.

[385]

Form III

The Leader and People pray responsively

Father, we pray for your holy Catholic Church;
That we all may be one.

Grant that every member of the Church may truly and humbly serve you;
That your Name may be glorified by all people.

We pray for all bishops, priests, and deacons;
That they may be faithful ministers of your Word and Sacraments.

We pray for all who govern and hold authority in the nations of the world;
That there may be justice and peace on the earth.

Give us grace to do your will in all that we undertake;
That our works may find favor in your sight.

Have compassion on those who suffer from any grief or trouble;
That they may be delivered from their distress.

Give to the departed eternal rest;
Let light perpetual shine upon them.

We praise you for your saints who have entered into joy;
May we also come to share in your heavenly kingdom.

Let us pray for our own needs and those of others.

Silence

The People may add their own petitions.

The Celebrant adds a concluding Collect.

[387]

Form IV

Deacon or other leader

Let us pray for the Church and for the world.

Grant, Almighty God, that all who confess your Name may be united in your truth, live together in your love, and reveal your glory in the world.

Silence

Lord, in your mercy
Hear our prayer.

Guide the people of this land, and of all the nations, in the ways of justice and peace; that we may honor one another and serve the common good.

Silence

Lord, in your mercy
Hear our prayer.

Give us all a reverence for the earth as your own creation, that we may use its resources rightly in the service of others and to your honor and glory.

Silence

Lord, in your mercy
Hear our prayer.

Bless all whose lives are closely linked with ours, and grant that we may serve Christ in them, and love one another as he loves us.

Silence

Lord, in your mercy
Hear our prayer.

Comfort and heal all those who suffer in body, mind, or spirit; give them courage and hope in their troubles, and bring them the joy of your salvation.

Silence

Lord, in your mercy
Hear our prayer.

We commend to your mercy all who have died, that your will for them may be fulfilled; and we pray that we may share with all your saints in your eternal kingdom.

Silence

Lord, in your mercy
Hear our prayer.

The Celebrant adds a concluding Collect.

[388]

Form v

Deacon or other leader

In peace, let us pray to the Lord, saying, "Lord, have mercy" (*or* "Kyrie eleison").

For the holy Church of God, that it may be filled with truth and love, and be found without fault at the day of your coming, we pray to you, O Lord.

Here and after every petition the People respond

Kyrie eleison.   *or*   *Lord, have mercy.*

For N. our Presiding Bishop, for N. (N.) our own bishop(s), for all bishops and other ministers, and for all the holy people of God, we pray to you, O Lord.

For all who fear God and believe in you, Lord Christ, that our divisions may cease, and that all may be one as you and the Father are one, we pray to you, O Lord.

For the mission of the Church, that in faithful witness it may preach the Gospel to the ends of the earth, we pray to you, O Lord.

For those who do not yet believe, and for those who have lost their faith, that they may receive the light of the Gospel, we pray to you, O Lord.

For the peace of the world, that a spirit of respect and forbearance may grow among nations and peoples, we pray to you, O Lord.

For those in positions of public trust (especially _____), that they may serve justice, and promote the dignity and freedom of every person, we pray to you, O Lord.

For all who live and work in this community (especially _____), we pray to you, O Lord.

For a blessing upon all human labor, and for the right use of the riches of creation, that the world may be freed from poverty, famine, and disaster, we pray to you, O Lord.

For the poor, the persecuted, the sick, and all who suffer; for refugees, prisoners, and all who are in danger; that they may be relieved and protected, we pray to you, O Lord.

For this *congregation* (for those who are present, and for those who are absent), that we may be delivered from hardness of heart, and show forth your glory in all that we do, we pray to you, O Lord.

For our enemies and those who wish us harm; and for all whom we have injured or offended, we pray to you, O Lord.

For ourselves; for the forgiveness of our sins, and for the grace of the Holy Spirit to amend our lives, we pray to you, O Lord.

For all who have commended themselves to our prayers; for our families, friends, and neighbors; that being freed from anxiety, they may live in joy, peace, and health, we pray to you, O Lord.

For _____ , we pray to you, O Lord.

For all who have died in the communion of your Church, and those whose faith is known to you alone, that, with all the saints, they may have rest in that place where there is no pain or grief, but life eternal, we pray to you, O Lord.

Rejoicing in the fellowship of [the ever-blessed Virgin Mary, (*blessed N.*) and] all the saints, let us commend ourselves, and one another, and all our life to Christ our God.
To you, O Lord our God.

Silence

The Celebrant adds a concluding Collect, or the following Doxology

For yours is the majesty, O Father, Son, and Holy Spirit; yours is the kingdom and the power and the glory, now and for ever. *Amen.* [389]

Form VI

The Leader and People pray responsively

In peace, we pray to you, Lord God.

Silence

For all people in their daily life and work;
*For our families, friends, and neighbors, and for those who
are alone.*

For this community, the nation, and the world;
For all who work for justice, freedom, and peace.

For the just and proper use of your creation;
For the victims of hunger, fear, injustice, and oppression.

For all who are in danger, sorrow, or any kind of trouble;
*For those who minister to the sick, the friendless,
and the needy.*

For the peace and unity of the Church of God;
For all who proclaim the Gospel, and all who seek the Truth.

For [N. our Presiding Bishop, and N. (N.) our Bishop(s); and
for] all bishops and other ministers;
For all who serve God in his Church.

For the special needs and concerns of this congregation.

Silence

The People may add their own petitions

Hear us, Lord;
For your mercy is great.

We thank you, Lord, for all the blessings of this life.

Silence

The People may add their own thanksgivings

We will exalt you, O God our King;
And praise your Name for ever and ever.

We pray for all who have died, that they may have a place in your eternal kingdom.

Silence

The People may add their own petitions

Lord, let your loving-kindness be upon them;
Who put their trust in you.

We pray to you also for the forgiveness of our sins.

Silence may be kept.

Leader and People

Have mercy upon us, most merciful Father;
in your compassion forgive us our sins,
known and unknown,
things done and left undone;
and so uphold us by your Spirit
that we may live and serve you in newness of life,
to the honor and glory of your Name;
through Jesus Christ our Lord. *Amen.*

The Celebrant concludes with an absolution or a suitable Collect.

[392]

Form VII

The Deacon or other person appointed says

Let us pray for the whole state of Christ's Church and the world.

After each paragraph of this prayer, the People may make an appropriate response, as directed.

Almighty and everliving God, who in thy holy Word hast taught us to make prayers, and supplications, and to give thanks for all men: Receive these our prayers which we offer unto thy divine Majesty, beseeching thee to inspire continually the Universal Church with the spirit of truth, unity, and concord; and grant that all those who do confess thy holy Name may agree in the truth of thy holy Word, and live in unity and godly love.

Give grace, O heavenly Father, to all bishops and other ministers (especially _____), that they may, both by their life and doctrine, set forth thy true and lively Word, and rightly and duly administer thy holy Sacraments.

And to all thy people give thy heavenly grace, and especially to this congregation here present; that, with meek heart and due reverence, they may hear and receive thy holy Word, truly serving thee in holiness and righteousness all the days of their life.

We beseech thee also so to rule the hearts of those who bear the authority of government in this and every land (especially _____), that they may be led to wise decisions and right actions for the welfare and peace of the world.

Open, O Lord, the eyes of all people to behold thy gracious hand in all thy works, that, rejoicing in thy whole creation, they may honor thee with their substance, and be faithful stewards of thy bounty.

And we most humbly beseech thee, of thy goodness, O Lord, to comfort and succor (_____ and) all those who, in this transitory life, are in trouble, sorrow, need, sickness, or any other adversity.

Additional petitions and thanksgivings may be included here.

And we also bless thy holy Name for all thy servants departed this life in thy faith and fear (especially _____), beseeching thee to grant them continual growth in thy love and service; and to grant us grace so to follow the good examples of (_____ and of) all thy saints, that with them we may be partakers of thy heavenly kingdom.

Grant these our prayers, O Father, for Jesus Christ's sake, our only Mediator and Advocate. *Amen.* [328]

A Bidding Prayer, form 1

Good Christian People, I bid your prayers for Christ's holy Catholic Church, the blessed company of all faithful people; that it may please God to confirm and strengthen it in purity of faith, in holiness of life, and in perfectness of love, and to restore to it the witness of visible unity; and more especially for that branch of the same planted by God in this land, whereof we are members; that in all things it may work according to God's will, serve him faithfully, and worship him acceptably.

Ye shall pray for the President of these United States, and for the Governor of this State, and for all that are in authority; that all, and every one of them, may serve truly in their several callings to the glory of God, and the edifying and well-governing of the people, remembering the account they shall be called upon to give at the last great day.

Ye shall also pray for the ministers of God's Holy Word and Sacraments; for Bishops (*and herein more especially for the Bishop of this Diocese*), that they may minister faithfully and wisely the discipline of Christ; likewise for all Priests and Deacons (*and herein more especially for the Clergy here residing*), that they may shine as lights in the world, and in all things may adorn the doctrine of God our Savior.

And ye shall pray for a due supply of persons fitted to serve God in the Ministry and in the State; and to that end, as well as for the good education of all the youth of this land, ye shall pray for all schools, colleges, and seminaries of sound and godly learning, and for all whose hands are open for their maintenance; that whatsoever tends to the advancement of true religion and useful learning may for ever flourish and abound.

Ye shall pray for all the people of these United States, that they may live in the true faith and fear of God, and in brotherly charity one towards another.

Ye shall pray also for all who travel by land, sea, or air; for all prisoners and captives; for all who are in sickness or in sorrow; for all who have fallen into grievous sin; for all who, through temptation, ignorance, helplessness, grief, trouble, dread, or the near approach of death, especially need our prayers.

Ye shall also praise God for rain and sunshine; for the fruits of the earth; for the products of all honest industry; and for all his good gifts, temporal and spiritual, to us and to all men.

Finally, ye shall yield unto God most high praise and hearty thanks for the wonderful grace and virtue declared in all his saints, who have been the choice vessels of his grace and the lights of the world in their several generations; and pray unto God, that we may have grace to direct our lives after their good examples; that, this life ended, we may be made partakers with them of the glorious resurrection, and the life everlasting.

And now, brethren, summing up all our petitions, and all our thanksgivings, in the words which Christ hath taught us, we make bold to say,

Our Father, who art in heaven, Hallowed be thy Name. Thy kingdom come. Thy will be done, On earth as it is in heaven. Give us this day our daily bread. And forgive us our trespasses, As we forgive those who trespass against us. And lead us not into temptation, But deliver us from evil. For thine is the kingdom, and the power, and the glory, for ever and ever. *Amen.*   [28BCP, 47]

A Bidding Prayer for Advent

Dear People of God: In the season of Advent, it is our responsibility and joy to prepare ourselves to hear once more the message of the angels, to go to Bethlehem and see the Son of God lying in a manger.

Let us hear and heed in Holy Scripture the story of God's loving purpose from the time of our rebellion against him until the glorious redemption brought to us by his holy Child Jesus, and let us look forward to the yearly remembrance of his birth with hymns and songs of praise.

But first, let us pray for the needs of his whole world, for peace and justice on earth, for the unity and mission of the Church for which he died, and especially for his Church in our country and in this *city*.

And because he particularly loves them, let us remember in his name the poor and helpless, the cold, the hungry and the oppressed, the sick and those who mourn, the lonely and unloved, the aged and little children, as well as all those who do not know and love the Lord Jesus Christ.

Finally, let us remember before God his pure and lowly Mother, and that whole multitude which no one can number, whose hope was in the Word made flesh, and with whom, in Jesus, we are one for evermore.

And now, to sum up all these petitions, let us pray in the words which Christ himself has taught us, saying:

Our Father . . . .

The Almighty God bless us with his grace; Christ give us the joys of everlasting life; and to the fellowship of the citizens above may the King of angels bring us all. *Amen.*   [BOOS, 30]

A Bidding Prayer for Christmas Season

Dear People of God: In this Christmas Season, let it be our duty and delight to hear once more the message of the angels, to go to Bethlehem and see the Son of God lying in a manger.

Let us hear and heed in Holy Scripture the story of God's loving purpose from the time of our rebellion against him until the glorious redemption brought to us by his holy Child Jesus, and let us make this *place* glad with our carols of praise.

But first, let us pray for the needs of his whole world, for peace and justice on earth, for the unity and mission of the Church for which he died, and especially for his Church in our country and in this *city*.

And because he particularly loves them, let us remember in his name the poor and helpless, the cold, the hungry and the oppressed, the sick and those who mourn, the lonely and unloved, the aged and little children, as well as all those who do not know and love the Lord Jesus Christ.

Finally, let us remember before God his pure and lowly Mother, and that whole multitude which no one can number, whose hope was in the Word made flesh, and with whom, in Jesus, we are one for evermore.

And now, to sum up all these petitions, let us pray in the words which Christ himself has taught us, saying:

Our Father . . . .

The Almighty God bless us with his grace; Christ give us the joys of everlasting life; and to the fellowship of the citizens above, may the King of Angels bring us all. *Amen.*
[BOOS, 37]

A Bidding Prayer, form 11

Especially appropriate for Good Friday or retreats

All standing, the Deacon, or other person appointed, says to the people

Dear People of God: Our heavenly Father sent his Son into the world, not to condemn the world, but that the world through him might be saved; that all who believe in him might be delivered from the power of sin and death, and become heirs with him of everlasting life.

We pray, therefore, for people everywhere according to their needs.

In the biddings which follow, the indented petitions may be adapted by addition or omission, as appropriate, at the discretion of the Celebrant. The people may be directed to stand or kneel.

The biddings may be read by a Deacon or other person appointed. The Celebrant says the Collects.

Let us pray for the holy Catholic Church of Christ throughout the world;

    For its unity in witness and service
    For all bishops and other ministers and the people whom
       they serve
    For N., our Bishop, and all the people of this diocese
    For all Christians in this community
    For those about to be baptized (particularly _____)

That God will confirm his Church in faith, increase it in love, and preserve it in peace.

Silence

Almighty and everlasting God, by whose Spirit the whole body of your faithful people is governed and sanctified: Receive our supplications and prayers which we offer before you for all members of your holy Church, that in their vocation and ministry they may truly and devoutly serve you; through our Lord and Savior Jesus Christ. *Amen.*

Gracious God, the comfort of all who sorrow, the strength of all who suffer: Let the cry of those in misery and need come to you, that they may find your mercy present with them in all their afflictions; and give us, we pray, the strength to serve them for the sake of him who suffered for us, your Son Jesus Christ our Lord. *Amen.*

Let us pray for all who have not received the Gospel of Christ;

> For those who have never heard the word of salvation
> For those who have lost their faith
> For those hardened by sin or indifference
> For the contemptuous and the scornful
> For those who are enemies of the cross of Christ and
> persecutors of his disciples
> For those who in the name of Christ have persecuted others

That God will open their hearts to the truth, and lead them to faith and obedience.

Silence

Merciful God, Creator of all the peoples of the earth and lover of souls: Have compassion on all who do not know you as you are revealed in your Son Jesus Christ; let your Gospel be preached with grace and power to those who have not heard it; turn the hearts of those who resist it; and bring home to your fold those who have gone astray; that there may be one flock under one shepherd, Jesus Christ our Lord. *Amen.*

Let us commit ourselves to our God, and pray for the grace of a holy life, that, with all who have departed this world and have died in the peace of Christ, and those whose faith is known to God alone, we may be accounted worthy to enter into the fullness of the joy of our Lord, and receive the crown of life in the day of resurrection.

Silence

O God of unchangeable power and eternal light: Look favorably on your whole Church, that wonderful and sacred mystery; by the effectual working of your providence, carry out in tranquillity the plan of salvation; let the whole world see and know that things which were cast down are being raised up, and things which had grown old are being made new, and that all things are being brought to their perfection by him through whom all things were made, your Son Jesus Christ our Lord; who lives and reigns with you, in the unity of the Holy Spirit, one God, for ever and ever. *Amen.* [277]

Footnotes

1   Charles Price, Member Drafting Committee for Prayers and Thanksgivings of the Standing Liturgical Commission

2   E. Milner White, in *After the Third Collect*

3   Unknown, in *The Prayer Manual*

4   F.B. Macnutt, in *The Prayer Manual*; based on phrases of Archbishop Garbett

5   Virginia Harbour, Standing Liturgical Commission

6   1959 Canadian *Book of Common Prayer*, p. 55

7   J. Robert Zimmerman, Member Drafting Committee for Prayers and Thanksgivings of the Standing Liturgical Commission

8   1959 Canadian *Book of Common Prayer*, p. 54

9   1928 *Book of Common Prayer*

10 Charles Price, Standing Liturgical Commission

11 *The Kingdom, the Power and the Glory*, (1933) NO. 35

12 Francis J. Moore, *Prayers for All Occasions*

13 John Wallace Suter, *Prayers of the Spirit*

14 Robert N. Rodenmayer

15 *Prayers New and Old*, ed. by Clement W. Welsh

16 Canon Macnutt, *The Prayer Manual*

17 Reinhold Niebuhr, *Uncommon Prayers*, p. 33

18 Alex Patterson, *The Prayer Manual* (68)

19 Caroline Rose, Member Drafting Committee for Prayers and Thanksgivings of the Standing Liturgical Commission

20 Unknown

21 Ashton Oxenden, Bishop of Montreal (d. 1892)

22 The Church Army (U.S.A.)

23 After William Laud (d. 1645), Archbishop of Canterbury (1633-45). From *Prayers for Our Ministry* (1916)

24 Henry Sylvester Nash, *A Selection of the Prayers of Henry Sylvester Nash*, ed. by John W. Suter

25 A.S.T. Fisher, *An Anthology of Prayers*

26 Miles Lowell Yates, *Our Bounden Duty*, p. 107

27 *Prayers for the Church Service League*, The Protestant Episcopal Diocese of Massachusetts, p. 109

28 Saint Paul's Cathedral, London, from *Prayers in Ministry*, ed. by Canon Macnutt, p. 202

29 Brooke Bushong, CA

30 *The Book of Offices* (1949), The Church Pension Fund

31 An ancient collect

32 Robert Louis Stevenson (d. 1894)

33 *Book of Prayers*, ed. by Leon and Elfrieda McCauley, p. 36

34 Bishop Brent, *With God in Prayer* (1907)

35 *Gelasian* (adapted)

36 Derwent A. Suthers

37 Dr. Samuel Johnson

38 *Prayers for the Minister's Day*, The Pilgrim Press

39 *Parent's Prayers* (1953), compiled by Muriel Streitbert Curtis

40 Charles S. Martin (b. 1906)

41 Leslie S. Hunter, Bishop of Sheffield, *New Every Morning* (1936)

42 *Book of Prayers*, ed. by Leon and Elfrieda McCauley, p. 40

43 *Lutheran Manual of Prayer*

44 *Prayers for the Church Service League*, The Protestant Episcopal Diocese of Massachusetts

45 *Prayers New and Old*, p. 60

46 Richard M. Benson, SSJE

47 Richard Feller (b. 1919)

48 *Prayers for the Church Service League*, The Protestant Episcopal Diocese of Massachusetts, p. 54

49 *A Book of Prayers* (1957), ed. by John Heuss, p. 66

50 Arthur C.A. Hall (d. 1930), Bishop of Vermont (1894-1930), *Prayers for Our Ministry*, compiled by Bishop Davies

51 Psalm 19

52 *The Pastor's Prayerbook*, NO. 348, unknown

53 *Prayers Ancient and Modern*, W.H.H. Aitken

54 *The Pastor's Prayerbook*, NO. 330, unknown

55 Church of Ireland Prayer Book

56 *The Occasional Services*, The United Lutheran Church in America, p. 136

57 Henry Sylvester Nash

58 Psalm 145

59 *Book of Prayers for Church and Home* (347), John Wesley

60 *Book of Prayers* (1851)

61 *Let Us Pray*, The General Assembly of the Church of Scotland, p. 31

62 George Ridding, first Bishop of Southwell; *A Litany of Remembrance* from *George Ridding, Schoolmaster and Bishop,* by his wife Lady Laura Ridding, Edward Arnold, London, 1908, Appendix II, pp. 352-355; adapted by Rt. Rev. Charles Williams as "The Southwell Litany", published in an undated pamphlet by Forward Movement; revised by Charles Price and Massey H. Shepherd, Jr., Members Drafting Commission of Prayers and Thanksgivings of the Standing Liturgical Commission.

63 *Calendar of Prayer for Missions*, 1961-1962; *Overseas Mission Review*, vol. iv, no. 3, Whitsunday, 1959

64 Mozarabic Liturgy (c. 600)

Note

Footnote references relating to some prayers taken from The Pastor's Prayerbook, *Oxford University Press, New York, New York,* 1960 *are herewith traced to their original publishers:*

Oxford University Press (New York and London): *Our Bounden Duty,* for prayers by Miles Lowell Yates; *The Kingdom, the Power and the Glory,* edited by Dean Eric Milner-White.

Forward Movement Publications (Cincinnati, Ohio): *Prayers New and Old,* edited by Clement W. Welsh; *Prayers for All Occasions,* edited by Francis J. Moore; and *A Selection of the Prayers of Henry Sylvester Nash,* edited by John W. Suter.

Morehouse-Barlow Company (Wilton, Connecticut): *A Book of Prayers,* compiled by John Heuss; and *Parent's Prayers,* selected and written by Muriel Streitbert Curtis.

Longmans, Green & Co., Ltd. (London): *An Anthology of Prayers,* edited by A.S.T. Fisher.

A.R. Mowbray & Co., Ltd. (London): *The Prayer Manual* by Frederick B. Macnutt; and *After the Third Collect,* by Dean Milner-White.

The Pilgrim Press (Boston): *Prayers for the Minister's Day* (1946).

The Protestant Episcopal Diocese of Massachusetts: *Prayers for the Church Service League.*

The Church Pension Fund (New York): *The Book of Offices* (second edition, 1949).

The Church Army in the U.S.A. (New York): for a prayer written for their use.

The United Lutheran Church in America (New York): *Occasional Service Book.*

The Del Publishing Co., Inc. (New York): *Book of Prayers,* edited by Leon and Elfrieda McCauley.

John Wallace Suter, *Prayers of the Spirit*

Macrae Smith Co. (Philadelphia): *With God in Prayer,* by Charles Henry Brent.

The British Broadcasting Corporation (London): *New Every Morning* (1936, 1955).

Little, Brown and Co. (Boston): *Prayers Ancient and Modern,* selected by Mary Wilder Titeston.

Index